NEW WRITING SCOTLAND

NUMBER FOUR

Edited by
ALEXANDER SCOTT
and
CARL MACDOUGALL

Managing Editor
DAVID HEWITT

Association for Scottish Literary Studies

Published by the
Association for Scottish Literary Studies
c/o The Department of English, University of Aberdeen
Aberdeen AB9 2UB

First published 1986

© Association for Scottish Literary Studies

ISBN 0 9502629 8 6

The Association for Scottish Literary Studies acknowledges
with gratitude subsidy from the Scottish Arts Council
in the publication of this volume

Printed by AUP Aberdeen

CONTENTS

INTRODUCTION

Last year's editors welcomed 'work by new writers who have published little or nothing before now and yet have a remarkable maturity and confidence of voice as well as impressive technical skills.' We are pleased to do the same, while also welcoming new work by established writers.

We received submissions from over 450 individuals, including three full-length novels and six plays, which amounted to thousands of separate manuscripts. In fact, we received more submissions, and are publishing more acceptances, than any previous volume, and we would like to think this is further evidence of the anthology becoming established as an important outlet for new work. However, we cannot help but notice that there are fewer outlets for writers in Scotland, and we hope that what has been seen elsewhere as a sign of the times is no more than a temporary phenomenon. The more small magazines there are, the better the opportunities for new developments. *New Writing Scotland* has proved there is a reading public who are willing to buy an anthology of poetry and prose. We hope would-be magazine editors and publishers are able to tap into this seam.

If this year's submissions can be taken to indicate any sort of trend, then the short story is a flourishing form in Scotland. Over two-thirds of our story submissions came from women and though women's issues are certainly aired, it is more usual to find events explored from a woman's point of view. The stories share a heartening exploration of adult themes and a readiness to see personal experience as a starting point for fiction, no matter how painful or awkward these experiences may be. When the writer does this, the result is often a very moving piece of work. People, circumstances and incidents are often closely examined, but the narratives are well controlled and yield rewarding insights.

It is almost to be expected that this volume's poetry would be distinguished by its diversity. A varied range of subject matter, in all three of our languages, is carefully handled, often treated with wit and candour, and always freshly observed through an individualist's eye.

Alexander Scott

Glasgow, 1986

Carl MacDougall

NEW WRITING SCOTLAND

is published annually in October.
Contributions may be poetry, drama, short
fiction or other creative prose and may be
written in any of the languages of Scotland.
Contributors must be resident in Scotland,
or Scots by birth or upbringing.
Submissions should be sent by 31 January to:

The Managing Editor
New Writing Scotland
c/o the Department of English
University of Aberdeen
Aberdeen AB9 2UB

IONA McGREGOR

ON THE STREET WHERE YOU LIVE

'I don't object to the *word*,' I said to their mother. 'It's the writing. They may have scratched the roof of my car.'

Mrs McQuirrell was looking at me warily with her lower lip jutting out half an inch. She obviously hadn't decided yet which way to react.

In her own home she seemed too old to be the girls' mother. She was wearing the sort of flowery pinny you see in old *Picture Post* photos of munitions workers; she looked like a youngish Ena Sharples.

But she didn't live on The Street. She lived in my street, and her kids had written something controversial on the roof of my new car. My neighbours living above ground-floor level could read it too: the frost had glazed it into a semi-permanent slogan.

I'd noticed the word about 11 a.m. when I happened to go to one of the sittingroom windows. I was taking it easy: I had a day off in return for some evening overtime.

The snow had fallen softly all night, and now the temperature was plummetting. Already the slushy road had frozen into a maze of tread-marks and slippery bumps of ice. The few cars still parked by the kerb were roofed with pure, sparkling snow, all except one. Mine. Someone had blazoned the snow with a three-letter word.

I admit that I flinched. For a moment I even felt the whisper of a witch-hunt licking my heels.

Carla rang at eleven-thirty to say that she'd be dropping in at lunchtime. She'd forgotten some file of notes she needed for an afternoon lesson. I waited until she had lit a cigarette and then took her to the window.

'Have you seen that?'

But her mind was already occupied with sixth period Senior 2. She glanced at my car.

'Yobbos,' she said with a laugh. Sometimes Carla's social analysis is painfully simplistic. Then she saw my face and managed to disentangle herself from Higher Maths.

'You don't mind, do you?'

'Like Hell I do!'

'Well,' she said reasonably, 'take down a bucket of hot water and clean it off. No? Go and add " . . . is good," or "So what?" ' I gazed at her, as they say, stonily. 'Sorry.'

I waited for her to work through all these evasive reactions, and at last she said, 'Oh, do stop brooding, Ishbel. It's nothing! Some kid or other. They did it for a joke.'

'Look,' I said, 'I don't like it. Got it? *I do not like it.*'

'You're not living here on your own,' replied Carla with a touch of sharpness. 'It affects me as well, you know. Rise above it. That's what I had to do, when 2b started scratching "Miss Sanders is a lemon" on their desks. *And* the Principal Teacher of Classics couldn't wait to get it to the Head.'

'You rose above it because you and John Malcolm came back from your boozy Advisers' meeting via the Regina Hotel, and you spotted your Head parked behind it in an extra-mural clinch with the Deputy Head's wife. You came to an agreement to split the difference . . . As far as *this* is concerned — ' I pointed down at my car — 'I think I ought to find out who did it and speak to their parents.'

'Don't be such an ass!' said Carla. 'It's only snow.' She looked at her watch and ground out the cigarette. 'I'll have to go. See you this evening, darling.'

I shut the door before she could reach it. 'Just *listen* to me for once. I object to having words written on my new car. I'd still make a fuss, even if it was only COW or BITCH.'

'That would be equally silly.'

I was not prepared to let it go. 'Don't you see, I have to do something about it just because it *is* that particular word? I'd much rather ignore the whole thing. But I won't be put off just because the label sticks.'

Carla sighed and sat down again. 'This is a load of crap. The trouble with you is that you work with books, you live and breathe books, and when a bit of real life pops up and says boo, you can't take it. You're always the same. You either over-react or you push it away altogether. I expect you've been like this all your life.'

'Not true,' I muttered. This was getting too near the bone.

'What's your most exciting experience in the last thirty years? Apart from meeting me, of course. Not happy or sad, just plain gut-heaving? When did the earth last move? Come on, Ishbel. Tell me.'

I thought deeply. 'When I was ten I came back from school one day and found that my cat had vanished. My father's C.O. complained that it kept going into the band-room and peeing over the percussion. He told my father to get rid of it. I was still howling over that cat two years later.'

'There you are!' said Carla triumphantly, pulling out another cigarette. Period 6 with Senior 2 had gone for sure. 'That's how far back you have to go. I'm sorry about your cat, darling, but don't you see how *unreal* your reactions are? Even when you were a teenager, you didn't get religion like the rest of us. You had to fall in love with George Eliot.'

'How can you get religion when you're being smothered by the Little Sisters of St. Ursula? Religion had already got me.'

With a name like Ishbel Pirelli, third-generation immi-grant, there's not much scope for expansion on the religious front.

'Anyway,' said Carla, and she stood up briskly, 'I really must go. My advice is, forget it. The whole place knows al-ready. They're not going to demonstrate under our windows, just because some kid has written GAY on top of your car.'

That afternoon in the kitchen I worried away at it as I stirred the macrobiotic rice. It was my week on as houseboy. Approach the problem logically: that's what I say to readers who wander helplessly round our reference section looking for something on nineteenth-century France. What type of information are you looking for? Political? Historical? Topo-graphical? (If they go on being vague, I know they're after the pornography.)

What I wanted to find out was who dun it. I took a god's eye view of the possibilities.

The community of Simmern-Zweibruck — named after some obscure German duchy of the pre-Bismarck era — is divided into S-Z Square, S-Z Street, and S-Z Crescent. We are a keyhole-shaped enclave of Georgian conversions, where a dozen life-styles battle to impose their tone on the area. The Square is at the top of the keyhole. In the Square the children are all called Julian or Arabella. They all seem to be under six. *They* couldn't have reached the roof of my car.

The uppitiness of the Square is only kept in check by the fact that its north side is taken up by a disastrous late-Victorian drill-hall. Other kids converge on it every night of the week for mini-bingo and majorette practice, and other non-Georgian activities. I know a lot of them by sight, but they don't know me. They're only passing traffic. If they have any time left over from counting the bingo loot, their graffiti usually begin with F. *They* wouldn't have written on my car.

Our flat looks across at Simmern-Zweibruck Street. And there aren't any kids at all living there.

But wait a moment . . . What about Robina Stewart? Our mid-fifties bush telegraph, directly opposite us? She's only on the first floor, which must rankle, but you can still spy out quite a lot from there if you work at it.

It was Robina who first informed Simmern-Zweibruck what was going on at 20 the Crescent, first flat left. Apparently the Lord spoke to Robina while we were wrapping up Christmas presents one evening on the sittingroom floor. We hadn't closed the shutters. Why should we? Last day for posting was yesterday, and we still hadn't settled which of our mothers should receive the calendar which neither of us liked. It's amazing what bad eyesight and a prurient imagination can make out of two people fighting over a role of sellotape.

For the next few days the older neighbours passed us with shuffle-eyed looks. Our private life is so private it took us that length of time to work it out. By then we had again blended into the scenery.

But no, I thought, it can't be Robina. She's timid as well as sly. She wouldn't like to be caught writing on someone's car.

Yet I couldn't think of anyone who might have done it, in our own Crescent either. For our teenage population, Carla and I weren't even yesterday's news. Besides, they were a bit old for that kind of hit-and-run malice. Yet it wasn't really malice. GAY hadn't been written to draw the eyes of the whole street to our windows: 'Here be Lesbians'. It must have come out of one child's dare to another, after a smutty giggle in a corner, something whispered behind sticky little fingers.

That afternoon I went downstairs to fetch a book I'd left in the car. As soon as I opened the front door I had the answer to my question.

On the top step were two small snowmen. I hadn't seen them from the sittingroom window. They must have appeared at the same time as the word on my car. The larger was about twelve inches high. They had twig buttons but no other decoration; the snow had been moulded to give them those blind-looking foetal eyes. Each nose was a delicate proboscis patted round a curved stick. They were facing the door. Their noses seemed to twitch expectantly.

'Oh,' I said. Two of them. And then I was sure I knew who had defaced the indifferent snow.

So here I was half-way along Mrs McQuirrell's basement hall. When I'd put the question to her, she had left me standing on the doorstep while she disappeared into the kitchen.

'Aye, it was them,' she came back to say. 'You'd best come in.'

She walked stiffly ahead, then stopped and said, 'It wouldna be Karen.'

At that stage it seemed brutal to crack the whole weight of it over Marilyn's head, so I replied, 'I don't object to the *word*. It's the writing. They may have scratched the roof of my car.'

Mrs McQuirrell led me along the well-waxed vinyl into the kitchen: the old iron range and every bit of Georgian brasswork were polished to death. The Conservation Committee would have been proud of her. There were two crinoline ladies on the mantelpiece and a Coronation mug. I felt I'd fallen into a time-warp.

Karen and Marilyn were swinging their legs on a battered chaise longue: probably wriggling with itchiness, because the horse hair was oozing out all over it. They were watching the afternoon Western. I wasn't tactless enough to ask why they weren't at school.

'Hello,' I said, as nonchly as I could.

Karen removed her thumb from her mouth and stopped rocking for a moment.

' 'Lo,' she said. She was the younger, eight years old, but small for her age, with a precocious look. She was a real little beauty, and knew it. Obviously she took after the long-vanished Mr McQuirrell.

I bet it *was* her, I thought; but she got her sister to stretch up and write the word.

Marilyn swivelled round to look at me without speaking. Then she returned to John Wayne.

I knew quite a lot about the two girls because a friend of Carla's was Marilyn's class teacher. Marilyn couldn't concentrate on anything for more that ten minutes. She was very soft-hearted: her huge vacant eyes flooded at the slightest jab to her feelings. This was rarely personal: she was slow to notice the cruel baiting that her school-mates inflicted on her. Besides, she couldn't bear anyone coming too near her.

Out of sheer panic she'd deal out a hefty right punch if the tormentors buzzed too closely round her. Her tears usually dripped over the dead birds she found in the playground.

Our local minister once called in to explain the meaning of Easter to Marilyn's class. Marilyn's total incomprehension had stirred up the missionary zeal in the Rev. Ian Mackie. For thirty minutes he wrestled to explain the link between Christmas and the mysteries of the Passion. Marilyn flopped over the desk and bawled her heart out. All they could get out of her was, 'Fancy crucifying a wee baby!'

Mrs McQuirrell now stared at me suspiciously across the kitchen table. 'I hope they're no being a problem, Miss Pirelli.'

She meant that I was being a problem. Up in the Square my complaint would have gone through all the paces of a well-regulated duel. This was jungle country. The animals were peering through the leaves. They weren't hostile yet. They'd wait for me to make the moves, and then they'd see.

But now I'd set the situation up I didn't know what to do with it. I glanced at the two girls and back at their mother.

'Could you please explain to Marilyn and Karen that they shouldn't write on people's cars. I know it's only a game, but it might scratch the paintwork.' I was using that fatuous voice that adults adopt when they're trying to get at children through their parents. 'That's all, Mrs McQuirrell,' I finished appeasingly. A tense knot in my stomach relaxed. I hadn't noticed it before. Mother Mary, let me get out of this as quickly as possible.

Mrs McQuirrell glared at her daughters. 'I'll belt them and they'll not do it again,' she said, but mechanically. Karen and Marilyn looked unimpressed. I wondered if the threat was a ritual or whether they got belted all the time. Karen's eyes glinted. Marilyn's mouth was hanging open.

'Oh,' I said hastily, 'just a word — eh — a talk with them would be enough, wouldn't it?' I smiled encouragingly at the girls. Mrs McQuirrell's face became troubled.

'Was it a bad word, like? I mean, one of they dirty ones? It's awfy what they pick up at the school. I dinna let them write dirty words in the house.'

I tried to synchronize my voice with a casual laugh, but the laugh came first and gagged my throat. 'Oh — well — you know — they wrote GAY.'

'Gay?' She assembled the word slowly. 'That's gey queer. How would they write that? Does it mean something special, like?'

I couldn't believe it. She was having me on. It had to be some kind of crude revenge. But no: sincere bewilderment gawped from her whole face. She was too busy cleaning that spotless kitchen to take in the misinformation handed out by the telly and the tabloids.

Mrs McQuirrell sat down at the table and pushed her packet of fags towards me. She waited.

'Gay,' I said, 'means — ah, queer, bent.' She was baffled. 'You know,' I pressed on, 'dyke, Lesbian.' I was still not getting through. Karen was sniggering; Marilyn's blue eyes were troubled. She had picked up some distress signal, but she had no more idea than her mother what was going on.

I said desperately, 'It means homosexual, Mrs McQuirrell.'

Relief relaxed her face — relief that she had understood. 'Oh ... I see. I didna ken. Fancy that!' Then her mouth pouted indignantly. 'My God, Miss Pirelli, who'd say that about you? Folk are awfy. And telling my wee lassies! You canna trust naebody these days.'

'Yes, but — ' I began. Things were getting out of control. I wish I'd left Carla to handle this, I thought. Then I remembered Carla had wanted neither of us to handle it.

Mrs McQuirrell lifted the teapot that was stewing on the range.

'Sit down, hen ... D'you ken this, I blame it all on the mothers that goes out to work. Me, I've never done that. Then there was yon poor wee lassie at Portobello. Have a cup of tea, Miss Pirelli. I'd hang the lot of them, so I would. And it dirties folks' minds, just hearing talk about it. Will you have a shortbread?'

'Thanks,' I choked over the rusty brew. I was paralysed. The jungle had put me in a cage.

Mrs McQuirrell blew smoke rings up to the ceiling. 'Fancy saying a thing like that about you! Right wicked, so it is. Never you mind, hen. We'll show them. I'll no let them fling muck at you. You've been right kind to me and the lassies. I mind how you lifted yon mattress out of the yard when I had my sore back.'

'That was nothing.' I remembered the white face and her knuckles battering at her kitchen window as the rubbish lorry churned along our street.

Mrs McQuirrell was thinking. 'You just listen to me. I canna bide at home for Marilyn's walk. I aye do for my mother on Sunday forenoons. I trust you, Miss Pirelli. I dinna heed what they say. Snotty-nosed bitches! You can take

Marilyn for me.'

'What's this? On Sunday, you said?'

'Aye, it's a sponsor, like. For the stray cats' home. They got it at school. The big yins are walking along Princes Street, but I just telt Marilyn she could walk round the Square.'

'I don't know if I can — .'

'Ach, it's just a wee doddle! She's signed up for twenty times round. My mother would caa me for a' thing. You dae it, hen. Karen will chum the both of you along. Will you no, my wee pet? And Marilyn's awfy keen. I dinna want to disappoint her. Miss Pirelli will come with you, my pets.'

The two heads nodded eagerly. Karen was sucking her thumb again, and I was sure she was smirking behind it.

'What's more,' I said to Carla that evening, 'Uncle Jimmy's pooch is coming with us. I wonder how a cairn feels about sponsoring stray cats?'

'Darling,' said Carla, 'you mustn't look a gift-dog in the mouth. Mrs McQuirrell is showing her confidence that we aren't into bestiality.'

I did the Sunday walk, or part of it. I gave up on round nine, clocking up the other rounds for Marilyn and Karen while sitting on a bench in the gardens. The cairn came to sit beside me after round ten.

On Sunday evening it snowed again. I had Monday morning off.

'Drive carefully,' I said to Carla as she picked up her car-keys after breakfast. I went to the sittingroom window to see how bad it was.

The kids on their way to school were having a great time — shrieking with excitment as they snowballed and slid along the pavement. The two McQuirrells were down there — and they were writing on my car again! Karen was on tiptoe over the bonnet, and Marilyn, very slowly, was completing the phrase across the roof. They looked up, saw me, and waved frantically. Karen blew me a kiss.

This time they had written:

                    WELIKEQUEERS

JANE WEBSTER

THE UNICORN DANCE

The unicorn was waiting, poised, fire beginning to contort the stone carved muscles. Behind him the sky blenched; dark clouds gathered and tore apart like a crowd beginning to riot. Soon it would be dark and then he would spring; leap from his roof-top to run through the empty streets, his hooves sparking nightmares from the ground, his eyes remembering the dreams that you forgot.

She was up in the graveyard, buzzed out of her mind. Behind her the wind screamed in the trees, and under her the ground bucked, slippy and treacherous with rain. The dead were awakening. They were rolling over in their sleep under the earth, rotting limbs reaching up towards her, skulls scraping against stone. The ground was splitting under her, breaking out in festering sores, trying to catch her out, throw her down into the morass of twisting, bodyless limbs.

But the unicorn was coming. She could feel him behind her, his hooves surging like the roar of a river, mane and tail cascading in a waterfall of light, huge eyes blazing. She got up, tried to run, tried to meet him.

And fell straight into Liz.

'Laini? Laini? Are you a'right? Christ, come on, we'd better get down the road.'

She was kept in the school for the rest of that week. Now she was older they treated her different. No great shouting matches now; they just told her that if she caused havoc like that in the school again they'd send her back to her mum and her problems. They meant it, too. She couldn't remember the havoc but everyone said it had been pretty bad, lassies as well as staff. She was sorry about that.

She didn't really mind being kept in the school. It was annoying like, not being able to nip out to the shop when you felt like it, but then she'd never been much of a one for going out anyway. As the staff said, she only went out when there was trouble.

Liz did mind. Very much. But then Liz did like to go out at night. She had a fella down the town, Spikes. Not that that was her real boyfriend; she only went out with him on weekdays. Her real boyfriend was called Toddy and lived through in Glasgow. Laini didn't understand it at all, but she liked Liz.

Everybody had been surprised when they palled up together. The staff all said it was a good thing; that she could learn a lot from Liz, and Liz could learn a lot from her. They meant that she could learn from Liz about make-up and hair and boys and things like that. Hell knows what Liz was supposed to learn from her.

Certainly the staff hadn't meant her to teach Liz about buzzing it in graveyards on stormy nights.

She decided to spend her time drawing the unicorn; just as he was, sitting on his roof-top. That pleased the staff; they even let her into the grounds so she could see him. But he wasn't the same. It was only at night that he started to live. By day he was just a little stone unicorn perched haphazard amongst the jumble of steeples and gables that was the old town. But by some magic just before dark he was the only thing left; a stone horse thrown against the sky like a statement; the first thing in the world and the last left.

Liz wasn't even allowed into the grounds. The staff didn't trust her, and bloody right they were too. Not that she said that to Liz. Spikes was hanging about; he'd just have to give Liz the wink and she'd be off, promises scattered behind her like confetti.

She didn't like Spikes. She didn't like the way he looked at her, or the way he strutted up and down the road like an over-fed cockerel. While she was drawing the unicorn he kept nodding and winking at her, trying to get her to come over. She just ignored him; damned if she was getting herself slapped on supervision for that stupid prick. He shouted at her, eventually; the staff heard that, and she was called in. She was quite glad, too.

Liz wasn't.

'You should have gone over and spoken to him, Laini.'

'Why? He wants to speak to me he can cross the road and speak to me, can't he? Or has he got bad legs, that he walks like that?'

'Laini, you dinnae have a clue. You cannae expect a fella to go running around after you like that.'

'I don't want him running after me at all.'

'But I do. And see if you dinnae speak to him, he'll think I'm no speaking to him, and he'll go off with that cow Lisa. I ken he will. Go on and speak to him next time, Laini, please. Tell him I'm asking for him all the time and I'll see him at the bus station Friday. Go on. Please.'

'If he's going to get off with Lisa just because you're no around for two days he's no worth bothering about, is he?'

'Christ, Laini, you just dinnae have a bloody clue, do you? Men are different from us.'

'That's a load of shit. Honest, Liz, you'd never let another lassie treat you the way he does. You're daft.'

'I ken. But it's different. Go on, Laini, please. Or I'll go on the run tonight and see him myself.'

In the end they compromised, and Liz wrote a note, which Laini agreed to deliver. Actually, Liz wrote several notes, as Laini refused to be party to the first three. Liz had to settle for telling him she loved him, without being explicit about how she wanted to demonstrate it.

'Don't know why you're bothering. Are you sure he can read? Looks too bloody gormless to me.'

'Dinnae get wide with me, Laini. There's more important things than being clever.'

'Oh aye. What?'

'Being loved.'

The note burned in her pocket like a hastily hidden cigarette. It spoiled the whole day for her. She hadn't even wanted to get out of her bed in the morning, and she was crabbit with everybody. And then daft Sally made it even worse by hauling her out of class.

'What's wrong with you, Laini? You're like a cat on a hot tin roof this morning.'

'Nothing!'

'Nothing? It must be something. Is your period maybe due?'

'Ach Sally! That's just like you. You blame everything on bloody periods. Nothing! Nothing! Nothing! Nothing is wrong with me, right?'

'Well don't take it out on me and the rest of the class then. Right?'

'Right.'

But nothing would stop the day turning round to evening, and Liz wouldn't let her out of it, now. So she went to draw the unicorn, glowering.

Of course he put in an appearance. He would. There he was, strutting up and down, ghetto blaster in hand blasting away. He'd seen her too, kept leering at her as if he thought she was just dying to have a closer gawk at him.

There was no way she was going to be able to do this. Her face was burning already. And sitting out here pretending to draw was a bloody farce. It would be better just to go in and tell Liz to bloody piss off and sort out her own love-life. And then she was on her feet and had her stuff picked up before she knew it, like a puppet jerked up by its strings. Like an avenging angel she tore down to the wall before her feet had a chance to take her back to the school.

'Oi! You! Spikes!'

He jumped, then grinned and started sauntering over towards her. But she didn't give him a chance to get there.

'That's for you. From Liz', she said, throwing the note at him like a grenade. It hit him right in the face, which she hadn't intended, but she wasn't hanging about to see him read it. She'd never been so glad to get in the school in her whole life.

Liz couldn't wait to get her alone.

'Did you give it to him?'

'Of course I bloody gave it to him. I said I would, didn't I?'

'Oh Laini! You're a wee gem, you really are. What did he say?'

'Say?'

'Aye. What did he say when he got the note? Is he meeting me or is he no?'

'I don't know.'

'Did he no say anything, like?'

'I don't know. I couldn't bloody hang about with the staff watching out the windows, could I?'

'Ach Laini! You could've talked to him.'

'Could I nick. And the next time give him your bloody notes yourself.'

So Liz shut up, but from the look in her eyes Laini could tell that she hadn't quite finished with her.

The unicorn was finished, and hung up on the staff room walls. She'd drawn him in black on red cardboard. But she'd got him all wrong; he wasn't a unicorn at all, just a little horse with a horn stuck on his head. Not even a live horse;

one of these silly china ones that stared sightlessly at you from shop windows, or gathered dust in display cabinets, unwanted and unused.

'Why do you love Toddy?'

'Eh?'

It was Friday, before lunch. Liz was getting ready to go home, placing her eye make-up like an artist finishing a masterpiece, scared that one more touch would ruin it.

'Toddy? Why do I love Toddy? What put that in your head?'

'You keep saying you love him.'

'I do. But there's no reason why. I just love him, and I would whatever he did. So?'

'So.'

'See your problem, Laini? You think too much. Instead of sitting in here going off your nut thinking you should be getting out and about, meeting folk.'

'Maybe.'

'Shit! Now I've gone and smudged my mascara. That's all your fault, making me talk about love. Love. You should be doing it, Laini, not sitting talking about it. Why don't you come down the town with me and meet some of the laddies? Pud's no going with anybody the now.'

'No thanks.'

'See? You won't even try. That's just like you.'

Eyes perfected, lashes kept carefully apart, Liz dolloped thick green gel onto her hair, and started to rub it in, then stopped to watch herself and Laini in the mirror.

'See if you spiked your hair you'd look just like that lassie in The Thompson Twins, so you would. Honest, Laini, have you never been in love?'

'I still love my Ma, sort of.'

'That's no the same. You're lucky, but. I hate my bloody cow of a mother. See if it wasn't for Toddy? I'd be like you and never go home at all.'

The staff nipped her head all week-end.

'Come on, Laini, think. You are now sixteen. You could leave here now if you liked. You must leave here before the end of June. It's nearly May. Where are you going to go?'

'I don't know. I'll find something.'

'What?'

'Something. Dinnae bug me, Sue.'

'Somebody's got to bug you.'

But she paused, stared at the ground, fiddled with the chain around her neck, then resumed her attack.

'Look. Are you still wanting to go home?'

'No. No. You ken that doesn't work, Sue.'

'Yes. I know. And you know. But you still want it, don't you?'

'No. I've told you, no!'

Another pause. This time Sue lit a cigarette, the match flaring loud in the silence.

'What's wrong with going to look at the hostel?'

'Would you live in a bloody hostel?'

'Yes. If I was in your position, I would. I'd at least live there while I got a job and found somewhere else to live.'

The silence was so long this time that Laini thought Sue had finished, judged it safe to look up. Only to find the soft eyes focussed on hers, the voice lower now, almost pleading.

'Just go and look at it, Laini.'

Liz came back from the week-end with three cracked ribs, a cut lip, bruises from head to foot, and a filthy temper. Toddy had found out about Spikes.

She'd marched in bright enough, tried telling the staff she'd tripped down the stairs at home. They weren't letting her off with that, though. Laini waited for her in their room, tried to ignore the caterwauling coming from the office.

Liz wasn't quite so bright when she came out the office; quiet and quick-moving like she always was after arguments, only this time her movements were stiffer, trying to save her sore side. And as always it was the same ritual; clothes neatly hung away, bag back under her bed, fags hidden under the mattress. Then she was sitting at the dressing table, hands twitching over her make-up.

'I don't need any eyeshadow now, eh? They bruises will do fine instead. Still need mascara, but.'

'What happened?'

'Nothing much. Wish they'd all stop making such a fucking song and dance about it.'

Liz paused, studying herself in the mirror, then gingerly started to wipe off her blusher.

'I'm too pale for that one. Need to be sunfrost, instead. But see that bloody cow of a mother I've got, Laini? God help me, I swear I will never speak to her again as long as I live.'

'Your Ma? I thought it was Toddy . . . '

'Dinnae you start! Youz have all got it in for Toddy. He's my fella; if I want him charged, I'll have him charged, not her.'

'But Liz, your Ma's right! You cannae let a laddie go about hitting . . . '

'He didnae hit me; he pushed me down the stairs. Anyway, some bloody fool she looked when the polis came and I telt them no, I'd tripped over the cat and fallen down. They were welcome to charge the cat with assault and battery, like. So then the cow grassed, told them I'd been out with him all night and she wanted him done for underage.'

'You were with him all night?'

'Aye.'

'After he'd done that to you?'

Liz turned round then, stiffly because of her ribs, eyes glazed, lips curled back over her teeth.

'How d'you mean, after he'd done that? Listen. Laini; if he didnae love me he wouldnae be bothered about me going with Spikes, would he? No, listen! We talked it all out last night. He's going to start saving, and soon as I leave here we'll get married. Course we'll have to stay at his folks for a bit, then . . . '

'You're off your fucking head, Liz.'

The silence filled the room like a weight. Liz turned back to the mirror, started to clear away her make-up.

'And you ken what's happened to you, Laini? You've been stuck in this dump too long. You're getting like one of them.'

Liz folded her arms neatly on the dressing table, then laid her head on top of them and started to cry. Soundlessly; only the shaking of her shoulders let you know. It must really have hurt her ribs.

And Laini sat on her bed, felt the blood draining out of her, leaving her as useless and unwanted as the ink and cardboard unicorn.

Over the next few weeks Liz's bruises healed, she even started to laugh and joke again. But the friendship didn't.

They still shared a room together; were still speaking. But they never spoke about the things that mattered. Liz never mentioned Toddy or Spikes to her, and she never spoke to Liz about her Ma, or the hostel. Or her loneliness. And soon Liz started going out of an evening with Gail.

The staff said that Laini had learnt a lot from the friend-ship, but grown out of it. That was just like them; they thought people were like books or shoes, to be picked up and used when you felt like it, then thrown away and forgotten about when you'd finished.

Just like they'd forget about her when she went to the hostel.

Tomorrow they would take her to visit the hostel. In two weeks time she would go to the hostel. Of course they said she didn't have to go if she didn't like it. Only there was no-where else for her to go.

Outside it was raining. The wind was tearing at the trees, howling through the windows of the old building like bats in-to Dracula's castle.

It was her old nightmare again, only this time she wasn't buzzed up. This time it was for real. The walls of the school were being battered by malicious, leering ghosts, coming to laugh at her and drag her away to hell.

She went into the staff-room. Sue was sitting there, knit-ting away just like it was any normal night. On the opposite wall her unicorn pranced, smirking away. She hated that drawing, now.

Sue looked up, fingers and pins still flashing efficiently.

'Just remember, Laini, when you first came here we had to drag you up the drive. It won't be as bad as you think.'

She sat down for a bit, tried to hypnotise herself by watching the needles. But it was no use. She went out again, shutting the door quietly so Sue wouldn't notice.

The whole building seemed to be tensing itself, holding its breath before it screamed. Any second now the concrete under her feet was going to rip apart like paper and the walls would fall in, smothering her, smothering them all. And this time there wasn't going to be any miracle, no lovely white unicorn coming to save her.

Well it could just all happen without her. They could come to take her to the hostel tomorrow; she wouldn't be here.

She went out the fire-escape, jacket and moneyless. She could jump a train. And then she was out in the street, gasp-ing and spluttering as if she'd been pushed under a wave, her footsteps running after her, loud as panic.

Once she was safely away from the school she made her-self walk. People always noticed you more if you were running.

Already her jeans and jumper were soaked and clinging to her. A cloud must have burst right above her. It was murder even just trying to walk; no chance of them looking for her in this. She had time to hide in an archway while the worst of the thunderplump passed; time to get her breath back and stop her hands shaking. She lit a fag but the damp from her hands spread through the fine paper. Two draws and it crumbled. So she stood there, water still dripping from her hair and slithering over her face, and watched the rain.

It was some time before she realised she was staring at a unicorn. One she'd never noticed before; she must always have come past here too quickly.

It was old; much older even than the other carvings dotted around the town; even she could see that. So old that all the edges had blurred, and it was difficult even to tell that it was a unicorn. You couldn't tell the legs apart from the body now, but the neck was still there, and the horn, and the head. It gazed sightlessly down the street, indifferent to the water streaming down its back to ricochet off the ground below.

No lovely white miracle coming to save her. Just a lump of stone that someone had turned into a unicorn. And now the rain was turning it back into a lump of stone again. A wet lump of stone, and a wet lump of a lassie standing gawking at it, clutching a crumbled cigarette in her hand as if it were a talisman. Probably catching her death of cold, too.

If she sneaked back through her bedroom window and dumped her clothes in the dryer Sue might never notice she'd been out. She could tell her she'd been for a shower. And needn't say it had been cold.

Wet clothes chafing her skin like a penitent's sackcloth, she started back to the school.

PAT MOSEL

SEASONS OF SATISFACTION AND DISCONTENT

He mustn't ring the bell. Just don't ring the bell — that's all. The sheets are cool at last and the fan is shaking its head methodically; in fact, this is the same sense I get when I dunk my hot body in the sea. Yes, yes, the sound of the air-conditioning could make me think I'm in a sea cave, floating amongst white sheets, with the fan giving and taking its breeze, rhythmically, on my face. Rupert is away again. If he were here I wouldn't be able to imagine I was in a sea cave; instead, I'd be in bed with my husband, a bed-sheet draped over the hump of his body, a fan and an air-conditioner. Rupert's head on the pillow. I just know he is going to ring the bell. Why can't he be a good slave and wait patiently outside until I get out of bed and open the door. He doesn't do things like that because he's too aware. Aware of what? Himself, of course. That's all very well — I don't like people who grovel — but I have to be considered too. Right now I'm enjoying waking up slowly, pretending I'm in a sea cave, cocooned by the hum of the air-conditioner and the sun-coloured curtains. I should have no deadlines. Yet that bell about to be rung ... What should I wear today? The ironing was done yesterday so I've plenty of choice. Something which doesn't show I'm not wearing a bra — can't feel exactly free under the circumstances, although I would say it's practical to go without one in the tropics. The dog wants to go outside. I feel like wearing my shorts today but as I'm not going to the beach that would be a bit whimsical. Blessed breeze, fan breeze. What's the time? Not that the clock helps much — it's always fast or slow — I can never find out the *real* time here. The red dress, I think. Loose. Cool. Thin shoulder straps. Oh, for heaven's sake, can't he give me a few more minutes? He'll just have to wait. He rang the bell before I was ready.

'Jambo.' *Hello.* 'Habari?' *Yes, yes, what news?* 'Salaama.' *Peace be with you brother. He doesn't wait to hear how I am; doesn't treat me as a human being at all really, which in some ways is quite a relief. Doesn't tell me how he is either. And I do wonder. Not exactly how he is, but who he is and what he thinks. To start with, it's impossible to imagine any-one thinking in a language other than English.*

I watched him go into the kitchen and waited until he'd started crashing about a bit, the signal that the day's work has begun. As a general rule he doesn't make a noise with the crockery; it's the knives and forks he throws into the sink, in a heap, *clunk*, steel onto steel. Then the water comes shud-dering out of the taps. I seldom interfere in the morning. It's a difficult time of day for everybody.

The dog was bouncing around like a bit of flotsam, her bladder egging her on. We went out of the flat and down-stairs to the back yard. It *was* early I realized. There were still plenty of idle cars scattered about, lining the driveway, any-where but under the pigeons' tree. A woman in the down-stairs flat feeds pigeons for some reason and so they stay, monopolizing that tree which is as tall as our three-storeyed block of flats.Two of them loved and laid eggs among our balcony pot-plants last year. It was a bit of a nuisance because we couldn't water under the nest. Nevertheless, plants and baby pigeons survived. Green and purple and grey. His re-action was strange. He wanted to pitch the shiny white eggs over the balcony railing and he laughed when I told him not to touch them. It was almost as if he thought I was being weak-willed. It's the same with the geckos which I tried to explain to him are useful house guests as they eat insects. Al-though I've never seen those strange albino lizards doing any-thing but scuttling away. *He kills cockroaches with great glee.*

The dog, Fluke, was snuffling around near the gate in a vain search for her master. Usually she's knee-deep in ant-infested fish bones and fly-covered milk cartons, savouring the nauseating stench. I pulled her back from her sure route to the busy road, tossed her up in the air and cuddled her so that she wouldn't mind too much about going back upstairs. Or keep me waiting.

I didn't really expect breakfast to be ready as soon as I walked in the door but I did anticipate some progress. When I saw the table laden with nothing but the daily newspaper I felt a familiar impotence.

Glancing tolerantly through the kitchen doorway I watched him bending over the cooker, scraping away at burnt toast. For some reason his top priority in the mornings is to make toast under the grill, then he tackles the fruit (mangos or pawpaw), then the eggs. The toast, which is made with inferior bread anyway, is always rock-hard despite my injunctions to wrap it up in a tea-towel as soon as it is ready.

I sat down in an armchair with my newspaper. It was riddled with slogans. The cruel were the capitalists or the fascists and the kind were comrades. I've learned to put up with such blatant propaganda. The paper he reads is written in Swahili. They say that the political slogans are reserved for the English-language papers, but frankly I don't believe them. Anyway, he reads his paper avidly, puffing away at a cheap menthol cigarette while we're eating breakfast. I don't mind really.

Soon I was confronted with a mountain of scrambled egg and tomato. He doesn't seem to be too flexible about quantities; I am required to eat Rupert's portion in his absence. Which was impossible, so Fluke helped me.

One of the things I wish he wouldn't do is wear those ghastly shorts. It's not that they're patched and dirty that offends me: it's that they give him an image which collaborates with that insulting word 'houseboy' which is still in common use here and which I consciously avoid. At a guess he's over thirty-five and, therefore, most certainly not a boy.

A few weeks ago one of our overseas visitors left him a pair of shiny running shorts and he wore them to work for a few days. He was embarrassingly proud of his appearance during those days and I could understand what a relief it must have been to wear a piece of clothing which was intact, without a tear, without a patch. Yet he seemed over-dressed, his loins girded in shiny red cloth, an athlete, a jogger, crouched on the floor and swilling around soapy water.

He could hardly bear me to look at him. Whenever I addressed him his legs seemed to squirm around as if he would like to put them behind his back. In his eyes, which meet mine occasionally, there was an uneasy mixture of defensiveness and pride. I should have joked with him about those shorts — and I almost did but something made me hold back.

That something is my role as Madam. I must wear the right clothes for that too.

'Husseini, can you pika chai please.' *My Swahili is abominable; his English is improving.*

He'll take about half an hour to produce tea. To start with, the kettle on the gas cooker is slow, but also he has another sense of time.

It's this foreign concept of time which has brought me nearer to racism than anything else in this country. You can see it in the way people here walk.

They saunter in the sun.

I no longer find their movement sensual, no longer. Instead, it infuriates me, arouses in me an almost violent impatience. Watching it, I think only of aimlessness, hopelessness. Sometimes I imagine that there is an airborne, sun-coated drug in this country so that the more you breathe in this air the more doped you become. Until you fall into slow motion. Over the years, you wind down to a standstill — when your time is up.

'Husseini. Chai!'

I went through to the kitchen where the water in the kettle had worked itself into a frenzy of bubbles.

He was out dumping the rubbish.

What does he think of me? Madam. He, strolling in here every day, doing the work I don't want to do, breaking dishes if he wants revenge for an angry word, never saying no. Always, always doing what I say he should.

It can't be natural, for in traditional African society — as far as I know — the women are the workers. I've seen them on the inter-city roadsides, tough mamas, work gouged into their skin. The President reiterates that the country must lighten the load on its hard-working women in the fields. Ploughing the soil, bearing children. Harvesting the crop. Having another baby. Still the status is in man, in manhood. They're breaking the backs of their women, and I — I am drinking tea.

This government doesn't want me to work for money. The argument is that there are so many unemployed citizens that expatriate women must not be allowed to deprive 'the people' of jobs. Yet it is possible to deceive the powers that be, or bribe them. It is done.

That time he saw me leaping away from the nip of army ants, Husseini laughed.

We were green then.

He doesn't laugh at me any more.
I don't jump.

I once saw his home, in a village surrounded by city sub-
urbs. Driving him there one afternoon, I saw him living out a
fantasy. I was the chauffeuse. He sat back in the front passenger seat, not talking, not smoking, but breathing arrogance.
One knee was cocked upon the other and his elbow rested
on the car window. He smirked, anxious. He was sure his
triumph wouldn't last. Thus he sat and directed me to his
home, past the scudded football field with its startled patches
of grass and the market place where vegetables cost a fraction
of what we paid, past clusters of woolly-haired children,
through the narrow spaces between the homes of his neighbours. We drove over the bumps and dips that the rain had
formed, exciting the dust.

I saw a tin roof and cool mud walls. There was a verandah
supported by slight wooden poles, a passage which passed by
curtained openings to the light of the back door. Inside, I suspected there'd be some of our forgotten goods perched in
corners. I could imagine smoke from cooking fires. The extended family, moving between jobs. Photographs of mother
and father, framed, people smiling starchily. Dust on the
floor. Cloth over a chair. A low, basket-weave bed; a scarred,
wooden table. Short people and a tall, tall silence if I had
entered. To some, nothing at all.

He introduced me to his cousin, an orphan; to his sister,
mightily pregnant. They stood around the car, smiled and
looked.

I was sweating and Fluke was licking the salt off my legs.
*In the atmosphere between us today there are the seeds
of a request. Since he came to work for us the pattern of his
demands has changed. At first it was daily that he wanted
something — not food, but money or clothes. He thrust guilt
in my way. Then monthly. Now quarterly; seasons of satisfaction and discontent. He'll want again soon.*

I found his girlfriend a job soon after she had been to see
me, plaits sprouting all over her head, wearing a red and
orange kitenge. She sat feet together on the edge of the settee
during the interview, while he brought her tea, jam and bread
without asking me.

She behaved like a guest, and I suppose she was one.

Husseini took Fluke downstairs.

He has no great respect for Fluke, which I can understand for in this country a dog is regarded as either a means of protection or an extravagance.

Husseini has developed a certain flair for being at home in our flat. When he first came to us he appeared to think he had found a luxury nest. I think he had hit upon this mistaken idea, not so much in reaction to the relative poverty of his own home but as a result of being unemployed for over a year.

I surprised him one day when he was still nervous and gauche. I came home from shopping earlier than he had expected and discovered him lounging on the settee, fag in hand, our radio belching out a hardy African beat. He had taken Rupert's bush hat from its hook and now it was aslant on his fuzzy black head, propped up on the bridge of his nose. The ironing board stood at ease near the door, the red light on the iron blinking dimly.

There was something so contrived and inflated about this scene that I wanted to giggle, though I managed to stop myself.

When he realised I was there he froze for some moments then, slowly, so that I had to respect his self-control, he tipped off the hat, held it reverently in two hands and, easing himself out of the settee, he took the hat to the hook. Still moving slowly, he began to busy himself with the ironing.

Without malice, I moved across to the radio and turned down the blast before leaving the room.

After a decent interval, I came back to turn it off completely and took it away for my own use.

Some months later I surprised him again. Or, was it the other way around? Did he surprise me?

There had been an eruption of robberies in the city. Rich and poor alike were living on the alert. Amongst our friends tales of intrusion were a dinner party obsession; a child held hostage with a machine gun, a woman almost raped, a man coshed in the bushes, screams, defence, departure. *The rich strengthened their gates and locks.*

'Husseini, have you locked the door?'

What happened that day was that I started out for lunch beside a hotel swimming pool, only to discover when I was already on the road that I had forgotten to take any money. I turned back and let myself into the flat in the usual manner. Granted, I was wearing rubber sandals which make little sound on the stone floor. I went to the bedroom and locked the door before opening up the cupboard where we keep valuables and cash. I don't know where Hussseini was at the time but he couldn't have heard me come in.

With a wad of cash in my handbag, I opened the bedroom door . . . only to close it again, quickly. I'd seen two shadowy, nearly-naked men cross the light and slide into the spare bedroom. For a while I was paralysed. It was finally my turn. I was the next victim of armed robbery. Up until then my plan had been to shatter a window and scream for help but I reaised with horror that my voice had gone. After a silent fight my senses returned and though there was a drumming in my head, I recovered enough to experience a kind of delayed recognition of the patch on Husseini's shorts. It was, after all, unmistakable.

Emerging, with my dignity all but restored, I found Husseini creeping coyly out into the passage followed by the friend and bodyguard he had summonsed. He was making the peculiar glottal 'oops' sound he resorts to when things don't go quite as planned.

Then we laughed, great whoops of laughter.

Eventually he became very earnest and explained to me in my mother-tongue that, hearing noises in the bedroom, he had thought I was a thief.

Husseini always opens the door to visitors but he's extremely inconsistent in his style. He can be silent and intimidating, leaving guests hovering in the doorway while he comes to rouse me. He can also display a sudden effusiveness which might well make a stranger think he or she has rung the wrong bell. 'Karibu', he'll say — the Swahili word for 'welcome' — and beam steadily until he has extracted a smile.

The time of day when the tick of the clock surfaces and the heat is suffocating. Fluke on her back with her legs in the air, to catch a draught.

The inevitable happened. Husseini submitted a letter asking for another loan. He must have asked the village scribe to draft it for him.

Dear Sir ad Madam,

I have the hon our to submit this letter on the subject of a roofing loan.

For sometime now i have been doing my level best to construct a mud thatched house for my family. So far, foundation, walls and upper part have been finalized. What i fail to acquire on my own is the galvanized corrugated sheets as the rains ar just around the corner I appeal to you for a loan as stated above to enable me to finish my house.

I will repay it in instalments per you. I am looking forward to your paternal arsistance with confindence.

Thak you,
I remain sir,
Your's faith full servant,
Husseini Mkwawa

'Mzee' would sort it out, I told him. 'Mzee' is the term of respect I attach to Rupert when I'm trying to drag in support from somewhere.

The phrase 'paternal arsistance' has come back into my mind like the local propaganda.
A resonant error.

The kitchen door banged shut, as part of the daily ritual. 'Madam.' The word was uttered not as a command, nor as a call, but as a statement. My part of the ritual entails getting up, giving him money for the next morning's newspaper, letting him out, saying goodbye and locking the door behind him.

Each day I turn from the closed door and see that the flat has been cleaned, not spotless, not shining with soap and polish, simply brought to order. After a few hours Rupert and I manage to make it untidy enough to look as if we are living here.

I'm always relieved when Husseini has gone, and I'm just as thankful when he comes back.

His letter was on the table, a very ordinary sheet of creased, lined paper. I picked it up.

There is no evidence that it is the work of a village scribe. The mistakes are artful, and to spell 'acquire' correctly is difficult — even for an English person. This man Husseini could be a con trickster, a man deliberately having trouble with his 'n's.

Absurd thoughts, yet he has always shown greater ability than he gave himself credit for in the first place. A servant shouldn't be able to write a letter like this.

And now I have hit upon what has been troubling me — the surname he has used on this letter is not the same as the one on the reference he gave us, dated a year back.

I have confirmed that, and I am now wondering whether we are employing Husseini Mkwawa or Husseini Mwaipopo.

A shadow of leaf patterns is laid out on the ground below, cast on a dusty surface.

From a tree, a peice of paper; from a man, a letter.

I have heard of Africans using different names for different purposes, for work and home. I think myself into this position for a while — as far as I can. I conclude that he is using two names to preserve the Husseini who dares to try on his master's hat, who gives the Madam directions from the passenger seat of a car, who smokes a cheap menthol cigarette while we eat breakfast.

(Unless, of course, that reference isn't his.)

It's true that the rains are due and perfectly likely that his family does need a roof for their new home. I suppose that for me there is only one way to interpret this letter. He needs help.

From where I stood I could see half-empty tea cups littering the room.

ROBERT CRAWFORD

IN MY FATHER'S HOUSE ARE MANY MANSIONS

Rivers don't stop. Even the Aegean's
Clydebuilt by now in an age when videoed kookaburras
Chuckle round Kilmarnock, and John Lennon's shot
In a privileged hotel in Beijing.
In my Father's house
Are many mansions: Getty residences
Thrown up by shacks, blackhouses and tents
From a desert encampment, manses with wide glebes
Of mangoes and palm trees. Sweat browns inside
Dogcollars of archangels. Ads for Gordons Gin
Precede the Last Judgment. Angels looking
Like Blondie cover the screen.

April 1, Sunday; the boy pretends
To be the Church Officer, approaches the bathroom door
Mimicking the sound of farmer's boots, and growls
'Can I speak t'ye, Minister?' My grandfather comes
Santa-Claused with shaving foam, and lays his razor
On the kitchen table, uncovering
A kind of holy folly. Every night
There is drawing the curtain that closes off
The navvies from the women, and every morning
He comes to find it rent in twain.

Shrines in the corner. Grandmother screams
If you do not bow, this strange Catholicism
That came to the country with the French,
Building an artificial hill in Hanoi, placing
Grottoes there with statues, idols, drums and gongs.
There is no end to it, but she still remembers
Our king who was carried in a litter through the city
    streets . . .
The inevitable foreigners, their alphabets and wars, their
    mansions.
Ypres. The Somme. They promised a whole elephant —
Not even a plate of clear soup.

Sierra Leone and New York
Daunted by each other: those rooms in the sky
That obliterate the sky, the polygamous architecture
Of E.F. Hutton, the incomprehensible
Creoles of pizzerias. In my Father's house
Dirt roads extend into the bush, a weaver bird
Angles down towards its nest.

My Faither's houss hes monie chaumers. The Bible's
International as nylon. You are in Princeton
At the RENEW program, teaching calculus, 'God
's more reliable than algebra.' Drifting in the Derry mist
Like slow-motion shrapnel. Unrecognizable.
Looks like it must have been a nail bomb.

God is a melon. God is a mountain. God is love.
High on Mount Washington the funicular railway
Stops, passengers grab hold vertiginously.
In my Father's house are many mansions ...
The machinery starts again, hauling them further
From the Maoris, the Inuit, the parked limousines.

Somewhere in a lab at CERN Geneva
A theoretician discovers in Weinberg-Salaam
The clear blue Otago sky.

I turn in sleep. I have felt my country
Calling through the earth, in a cable that stretches
Through the very centre, fibre-optics
Piercing the magma. I have heard its voice
Singing, normal as a thrush.

It has called me with these words
Of Christmas in Glasgow, the angels' voices
Speaking to the shepherds surrounded by warm sounds of
     traffic
On a rainy night. I have woken among the many mansions
Cradling a word, the name of a country
Precise as an apricot, an absence held in the hand.

If it were not so, I would have told you.

Adobe, concrete, timber, brick, snow. In
My Father's house are many mansions, each
Prepared and waiting, no stranger than this earth.
Found at the roadside, at the start of a meal
Of bread and wine, or where highland cows
Clamber at evening through the specious eye of a needle,
REALTY, reality, Ballachulish, Tonkin
Returned to Sender, the Logos read and considered,
Gin a man luves me, he will heed my wurd,
Transported with a kind of Grace.

RAIN

A motorbike breaks down near Sanna in torrential rain,
Pouring loud enough to perforate limousines, long enough
To wash us to Belize. Partick's
Fish-scaled with wetness. Drips shower from foliage,
    cobbles, tourists
From New York and Dusseldorf at the tideline
Shoes lost in bogs, soaked in potholes, clarted with glaur.
An old woman is splashed by a bus. A gash
In cloud. Indians
Arrived this week to join their families and who do not feel
Scottish one inch push onwards into a drizzle
That gets heavy and vertical. Golf umbrellas
Come up like orchids on fast-forward film; exotic
Cagoules fluoresce nowhere, speckling a hillside, and
                                   plump
Off dykes and gutters, overflowing
Ditches, a granary of water drenches the shoulders
Of Goatfell and Schiehallion. Maps under perspex go
    bleary,
Spectacles clog, Strathclyde, Tayside, Dundee
Catch it, fingers spilling with water, oil-stained
As it comes down in sheets, blows
Where there are no trees, snow-wet, without thought of
    the morrow.
Weddings, prunes, abattoirs, strippers, Glen Nevis, snails
Blur in its democracy, down your back, on your breasts.
In Kilmarnock a child walks naked. A woman laughs.
In cars, in Tiree bedrooms, in caravans and tenements,
Couples sleeved in love, the gibbous Govan rain.

MAUD DEVINE

SUN WORSHIP

It's a re-run of Christmas
On the video
But I've seen the show
Choked on the smoke
Gagged on the cake
Decided to go
Take a felucca.
'Goodbye Santa,
Gone for a sail
Up the Nile.'
Caught a smile
From Tutankhamun
Out of his tomb
Always the gentleman
Clasping his asp
His polished gold mask
Shining in the sky
Beside the Horus eye.
It was murder in Heaven
Until the god had risen
Come back to earth
Fought the devil Seth
Frightened him to death
Blew a fierce simoon
Made the desert bloom.

I've enjoyed this land
Built castles in its sand.
It's my buried treasure
Where I can take the measure
Of winter, well hid
In my secret pyramid.

ROLAND PORTCHMOUTH

ODD ONE OUT

No one in our family has ever been famous for anything
outside the family. Inside the family, though, and among
    ourselves
there's more than one with quite a reputation
— the sort bought by Sunday newpapers and much admired
by amateur psychologists. Several of us would be well-
    known cases
if someone in the family had split on the rest;
but none of us has, tending rather
to dry up when things start leaking out. After all,
we run to largish numbers, and in any crowd
there's bound to be the homely lunatic or public nuisance,
the shameful and the shameless, the one with a flowery vest
under the pin-stripe suit, or a plastic apron
beneath the ocelot fur coat. There's always
the meek, retired gas fitter inflamed to insane vengeance
by one greenfly on his rose bush; and the bison-chested
    builder
who reads Pixie Frolics to his six infants after work
affecting all the different falsetto voices; and the pale
    antique lady
who accosts a diesel truck with rake and rancour
for stopping at her garden gate emitting dense fumes.
There's no doubt about it — a family as big as ours
hasn't a chance of being normal. Turn an uncle
and you'll find an auntie no one knew about; turn auntie
and you'll surprise three old railwaymen we always thought
left the district to improve themselves. Largely on account
of being a close family, we keep in touch and have no secrets
— which is probably the reason the less particular
invent a few.
        And that's the point:
        some quite distorted facts
have circulated recently it seems, and the time has come
for one of us to act responsibly. Because of this,
I'm disclaiming now any connection with it.

HARRIET SMYTH

IN BLUEBEARD'S CASTLE

Three weeks after Alan Ross was flung through the windscreen of the school minibus, David's mother walked into the loch at the edge of the town, and kept walking until the grey December water lapped over her.

The boy knew something awful had happened when his granny arrived, clasping and unclasping her hands. When she and his father took him into the sitting-room and told him about his mother, his first surge of emotion had left him with a moment of pure peace. Some secret he could not yet understand, which was just beyond his reach, had almost become apparent to him. For his mind had been in torment since he had heard that the minibus had skidded into a tree, killing Ross by hurling him through the windscreen. David had crept up to his room, and curling up under his quilt, had wept bitterly. His mind ceaselessly threw up the image of Ross being projected onto the road like a spat-out ball of spent bubble-gum.

In the days following, he had turned to his mother, expecting her to share in his grief for Ross; to somehow make the older boy's death explicable, bearable. But she had seemed unmoved. As he followed her miserably round the house on the day of Ross's funeral, he had seen her smile to herself several times. When other teachers from the school called on her, wanting to talk about Ross — his intelligence, his promise as a sportsman, his amazing maturity for a lad not yet eighteen — his mother had nodded, distant, seeming not really to care. Watching her, he had felt a fierce rage against her.

For David had quietly and privately worshipped Ross, the Head Boy of the school, but, to David, more man than boy. It wasn't just the set of Ross's body; his light-footed, agile strength which set him above the other Seniors. It was more the impression Ross gave of being in control; not just in control of his school duties, but in control of himself.

The worst thing about his mother not seeming to care, was that David felt sure that she and Ross had liked one-another. His thoughts had turned to Junior Assembly, where it was customary for the Head Boy to read the Lesson. He could still see Ross standing quietly on the platform, looking out over the restless rows of children. David had always kept an eye on his watch to see how many seconds it took before four hundred under-fifteens ceased to shuffle, chatter, punch and belch. Once his presence had drawn them into quietness, Ross would begin to read. He read as if words were the most important things in the world. To David, the hackneyed Bible stories seemed to become new. Especially when Ross laid aside the Bible and spoke the words direct, his eyes moving over the rows of younger children. When Ross spoke the Bible David believed. The rightness of the words made him have to fidget to stop his tears, and sometimes he had to rub his hands together in order to absorb the sweat which had sprung from his palms. At the end of the Lesson, Ross bent his head, as if in homage, and the congregation of children seemed to send out a great sigh of response. Then Ross would look across to David's mother, where she sat at the piano, and they would exchange a smile. The memory of the smiles and the recent, clear evidence of his mother's indifference to Ross's death, were a constant source of conflict in the boy's mind.

How could she have stayed away from Ross's funeral? How could she have allowed someone else to play the hymns? David knew Ross would have wanted it to be her. Whenever he thought of her callousness his chest seemed to swell up, and grief for Ross took him by the throat, threatening to stop his breath.

And then she had walked into the water.

On the day after she was lifted from the loch, David went into the small bedroom she had used as a study. Her exercise books, still unmarked, were laid face-down in a pile, their covers a pretty blue in the bright, cold winter light. Sitting at the desk, he could hear his granny down below, talking on and on at his father. He had picked up a paperback novel his mother might have been using with one of her classes. Under the little penguin he read, *The Glittering Prizes*. The cover showed a dark-haired man wearing a university scarf. The boy was about to replace the book, when he noticed the tip of a bookmark. Opening the novel he found himself looking at the final page. He saw a cross, in red marking ink, beside the very last paragraph. David read it to himself:

They asked him how he had managed for so long to lead a double life. He replied that nothing was easier. As long as he could keep just one chamber of his castle locked and its contents safe from scrutiny, Bluebeard was model husband, reliable father and responsible citizen.

When his granny called him, David tore the last page from the book, folded it into his pocket, and left his mother's room.

Later, lying on his bed re-reading the torn-out page, he thought of his mother in her classroom during lunch-break, sitting at her desk, marking or preparing the afternoon lessons. The first time he had sought her out had been during his first week at the school. He had felt very lonely after the small, secure world of his primary school. Standing on tiptoe to look through the glass panel in her door, he had seen her alone at her desk, head bent, writing. It was not until he was inside her classroom that he saw she was not alone. Ross was sitting by a window, legs stretched along the sill, gazing out and down into the playground.

During the next three months the boy had spent many lunch hours with his mother and Ross. She worked, Ross lay along the window sill, and he read or dreamed or did his homework. They seldom spoke; nothing ever happened; but it was the part of the day that David most looked forward to.

Half-way through his mother's funeral service, when the congregation had their heads bent in prayer, David, scanning the pews on his left, noticed the fair-haired woman. Like him, she was not even pretending to pray. Then he realised she was watching him, and he flushed and bent his head. After the prayer had ended, he glanced quickly across at the woman. She was wiping the face of a girl who sat next to her. David recognised the girl as one of his mother's pupils; a girl from Ross's year. In fact, the girl who had wanted to touch Ross.

David had been sitting in his mother's car, in the school car park, when he had seen the girl walking with Ross. It had been a beautiful afternoon, an Indian summer day. He had the car windows wound down, so he had heard Ross talking to the girl. Even now, he could not work out what it had all been about. The girl had seemed to want to hold Ross's hand; but Ross had pulled his arm away, and, as the laughing girl had grabbed at it, he had held his body away from her, thrusting at her with his elbows. Ross had looked angry, and David had heard him say, 'I don't like being handled!' The girl had laughed, grabbing Ross's belt and hanging on. Then Ross had begun to fight her, twisting and turning his body, unable to break her hold until he tripped her and sent her thudding to the ground.

David found that he had let himself slip almost to the floor of the car. He was trembling, and yet felt strangely exhilarated. When he sat up in the seat he saw the girl hurrying away, head bent. Ross was moving quickly over the playing fields, his shirt-tail very white against his dark trousers.

He turned away from the weeping girl, only half hearing the minister talking about his mother — saying something about her dedication, and her skills as a teacher. Why, he wondered, if Ross disliked being touched, had he let his mother touch him? For he had once seen her touching Ross; once, after a school cricket match. It was a Saturday afternoon. David and his mother had been alone in the school kitchen, she making pots of tea, he loading a trolley with cups and saucers. Ross had come into the kitchen, stripped to the waist, trailing his shirt over his shoulder. He had run the cold tap, then pushed his head under it, letting it run into his mouth then over his hair.

'Alan!' His mother had exclaimed, 'You should know better than that!' She had taken the shirt and begun to rub Ross all over, long strokes, as if he were a horse. Ross had closed his eyes and raised his arms above his head.

Then his mother had said, 'Golden Lad.' Ross had kept his eyes closed, but he had smiled. 'Chimney Sweeper', he answered.

David shook his head, as if the violent motion would help him to understand. Looking round, he saw the fair woman watching him again. She smiled a very small, tentative smile. The smile was the same smile he had just been holding in his mind. Ross's smile.

Outside the church, David looked around him, trying to see the woman again. Instead, he noticed his father and grandmother consulting together, and realised they had been coming to a decision — he was not to be allowed to come to the cemetery.

Before his father could speak, David said, 'I want to come.'

His granny started to protest, but his father put an arm around his shoulder and led him towards the line of waiting black cars.

When they reached the cemetery, it seemed to be in the grip of even colder weather than the rest of the town. The cinder paths were hard frozen. The gathering mourners crunched and slithered towards his mother's grave. David noticed a group of men under a tree, backs turned towards the mourners, smoking cigarettes. It was not until he saw what was under the green tarpaulin that he realised they were the grave diggers. He wondered how such a deep and perfect trench could be dug on such a frosty day.

His granny began to sob, clutching his head against her, when his mother's coffin was slowly lowered down. But it was not this sight which finally broke him; it was a much smaller part of the ritual, perhaps, for all he knew, not even a real part. For he saw one of the gravediggers, an elderly man, in shirt sleeves despite the weather, who bowed his head in a kind of homage. David felt a shock of recognition; and then a sense of profound and unbearable loss. He pulled away from his granny and began to push about among the close-packed mourners.

He started off whimpering 'Mummy, mummy.' Then it became 'Mama, mama', and he felt as if he were a small, toddling boy again. He had begun shouting it as he pushed out into a clear space. And there he found Ross's mother. He ran towards her, still shouting, 'Mama, mama!' The woman caught him in her arms and lifted him. She seemed to hold him as easily as if he were an infant.

His voice rose now, almost towards a scream. He heard himself and was afraid, for now the words were, 'Ross, Ross, Ross!' Over and over. He noticed everything around him very clearly; as if each image was a photograph put into his hand by an expert photographer. He saw the cloudless beauty of the sky; the trees like ink drawings; his Maths teacher sobbing loudly, half-bent, both hands over her face; and, as his last cry for Ross hit the air, a brown bird, which burst from a bush, screaming in reply.

Ross's mother walked swiftly, never stumbling, his arms around her neck, his legs dangling on either side of her body. By the time they reached the car he was no longer shouting, only clinging very tightly to the woman.

The driver helped Mrs Ross into the car and rearranged David's legs so that he could sit on her lap. The movement of the car made the boy turn his head, and he found his granny at his other side. He examined her face as if she were a stranger. His father, in the front seat, had turned round to take hold of his hand, and was gently stroking his wrist.

As the car moved noiselessly towards the main road, David, looking at the passing gravestones, remembered that Ross, too, had been buried here. He looked up then, into Ross's mother's face.

'I hope he's close to her,' he said.

And, as he heard himself saying these words, David, at last, felt he understood.

MARY GLADSTONE

A VINDICATION

Dear D,
   ... How should I begin, or should I be writing to him at all? I'm just one of the many he deals with; I doubt if he gives me a moment's thought from one week to the next ...

Dear D,
   Your letter of the 6th inst. was received yester ... Good God! To think that I call myself a writer; it reads more like a bank manager's letter. Come on, Rosamund, pull yourself together. Write one of your sensitive, literate letters to your publisher ...

Dear D,
   Thank you very much for sending me the proofs of my ... no, no, no; it's too obsequious. Who the hell does he think he is? He's just a scabby old editor, a writer manqué, a man who couldn't make it in a more competitive and less gentlemanly business, like a firm that produces underwear, gardening tools or maltesers ...

Dear D,
   I got your proofs yesterday. Thanks for sending them ... Now what did I hear on the radio the other day? Yes, I remember; it was a talk by a professor of English language at an east coast university who admonished writers, and other people who should know better, not to degenerate and deglorify our literary heritage by employing slang and contractions and all sorts of other heinous things in our writing. But what the hell! *You* can stand my breezy colloquialisms, can't you D? Wait a minute, though! I seem to recall that you're a stickler also for form and dignity. I remember vaguely that we had a lengthy argument once about whether I should be allowed to keep the word 'shite' in one of my earlier stories. Had I used it in straight narrative, I would have probably left the 'e' off the end. But I wanted my character, a feminist lesbian single-parent, to exclaim in the middle of the

story, which was located in the seedy end of the New Town
(somewhere between Broughton Street and Canonmills)
'shite'! Somehow I felt that the word with the 'e' on the end
added an extra dimension to the story.

But dear old D, down there in his Bloomsbury office
lined with leather-bound first editions, thought differently.
You wrote that you were '*so* sorry' (why do you always write
that you're *so* this and *so* that?) 'but we' (royal, of course)
'cannot include the word "shite" in your story. You see,
Rosamund, one has to realise that the word can still offend,
and one doesn't want to alienate the mass of the reading
public, does one?' To which I wanted to reply with a letter
containing one word, 'Balls!'

God preserve us from reasonable, liberal, understanding,
sympathetic, but covertly autocratic and manipulative editors
of publishing houses! But I'd better cool down. If I write a
diatribe I'll be showing you, D, how much I'm at your mercy,
that I hang on your every word, wait for your letters when
the post comes each day, that I am a writer who has fallen on
hard times, and hasn't much chance of getting away from
them . . .

Dear D,

As an unknown writer . . . no . . . a new writer, a tyro,
a beginner . . . no, no, I can't undermine myself like that. If I
do it to myself, how can I expect anyone else to think well of
me? What approach should I take? I mustn't be too concili-
atory, but neither must I appear conceited.

Dear D,

. . . this time I'll get it right! . . . Thank you for sending
the proofs of my story . . . that's okay . . . I am pleased
you have decided to publish my story, 'Dead Bricks', in your
forthcoming anthology of *New Writing*. When I last saw you
we discussed together the story so that you could edit it
properly, and I told you I didn't care a jot what you did to it.
I had moved on to other things, I said. I used the simile that
my stories, essays and poems were like paper darts which
were shot into the wind. Some landed on target; others didn't.
But that wasn't entirely true, D. I was trying to appear un-
concerned and nonchalant. I said I didn't care what you did
to the story, but in my heart of hearts I did. I cared passion-
ately. I was too frightened to say how strongly I felt about
the way you had butchered my prose. You know the bit here

in the proof, the bit you wrested from me, stirred around and regurgitated so that it resembled a thalidomide child. You bolted with my work. You said, of course, in your letter that you had to edit heavily my story to make it clear, to iron out the pieces of dialect that were incomprehensible, and the eccentric punctuation. Confound your metropolitan parochialism, D! Confound you in your leather-lined Bloomsbury haven. Those incomprehensible bits are the language of my home-town. You said that no-one would have understood my heroine if I allowed her to girn at the broo. And when she tripped in the close you thought I was writing Double-Dutch. Well, D, what about your Faulkner? Don't you, when he writes about rednecks and other Southern people, let him keep his vernacular? So in that case why can't you let me keep mine?

You had another reservation about my writing, didn't you D? You said it was essential that you lighten the load; my story was too dark and depressing for your kind of readership. You complained of the ending where my lesbian separatist single-mother takes a nose-dive, pram before her, from the top of Arthur's Seat because she could no longer tolerate the fact that her lover had left her to marry the Lord High Advocate and settle down in a detached house in Davidson's Mains. My writing was too subjective and emotional, you said. But, D, being subjective *is* valid; subjectivity is merely a microcosm of the whole world, is it not? When I protested, you just grumbled about the arrogance of writers and tried to humour me making me feel more impotent than I had felt before.

Do you remember when I first came to see you in your Bloomsbury sanctuary? Up until that point I addressed you as Mr T. Then you asked me to adopt that nice compromise between familiarity and formality, so I wrote to you as Dear DT. When you asked me to call you by your first name, I thought aha! This is it. I am at last admitted to the inner echelons of the revered world of men of letters even though I am a woman. How marvellous it is to live in the late twentieth century when one doesn't need to change one's name to George or Acton or Currer!

Do you remember, D, when you took me out to lunch? I won't forget those friendly avuncular admonitions of yours: Miss F, you called me at the hors d'oeuvre stage but by the time the dessert came round you had started to use my first name. You lectured me on your firm's fine tradition of

handling female writers; you said that they were good to have
on your list particularly the younger ones who could boast a
pretty snapshot on the end cover. But I protest strongly, D;
my vagina is as intelligent as my brain is pretty!

To get back to your reservations about the darkness in my
writing: 'Why must I dwell on the pain?' you remonstrate.
'Aren't there in life happy experiences and moments of joy?'
Of course there are, D, but like the poet, Anne Sexton, I feel
that pain engraves a deeper memory. It takes courage to write
about those dark areas, 'it's dangerous in there,' they say.
'It's wrong — even evil — to explore those skeletons.' But I
want to explore so I may understand; that's why I fossick
and exhume. 'Be a fool,' said Anne Sexton; that's what one
must be, and *that* takes courage. Do you understand, D? I've
always felt displaced and that I belong nowhere. I certainly
don't belong in your galley of quasi-fools, DT: those who
pander to commercialism and stick in the middle of the road.
By you, D, I am simultaneously respected and reviled: you
want what I produce (you applaud it wholeheartedly) but
you're not so keen on supporting my vagaries, as you call
them; you think I am haughty, wayward and recalcitrant.
Can't you see that I don't belong anywhere except perhaps
with the mad or the bad, but ultimately with the fools.

I think it was you, D, who implied that there was something unwholesome in conjuring up the dark spirits: 'don't
paint the devil on the wall', you said reminding me of an old
German adage. Maybe you're right, D. Who knows? I mustn't,
you intimated, engrave such obscenities on the human consciousness. I was even accused of conjuring them up from
the ether adding more dirt to the ever-flowing pool of mud.
But am I not merely reflecting our world but in an artistic
form?

Grim though my writing may be, my preoccupation with
misery and pain has a beauty of its own: as a writer once remarked when he first saw Calcutta, the city of the dreadful
night, poverty *is* picturesque; the truly hungry assume almost
balletic compositions; beggary *is* beautiful. The face of a friend
racked in pain while he was dying had a poignancy as frightful
and beautiful as the painting by Poussin of the 'Massacre of the
Innocents'. I can picture you moving uncomfortably in your
well-upholstered seat, D, the reasonable white liberal of
North West London that you are.

Why should I not be allowed to pick my scabs and examine them? I have no need to vindicate myself; haven't

those Christians for almost two thousand years flaunted shamelessly the model of the instrument of torture that murdered their leader, bejewelling it, hanging it proudly round their necks, placing it on graves and altars; is it not the most powerful symbol of the occident?

What I really want to say, D, is that anyone who enters new territory finds inevitably that he/she is alone and misunderstood. I may not be much of a harbinger, scout or whatever else you want to call an artist but I'm still up against that age-old problem besetting one of my kind: that what I choose to write about is generally thought of as an unfit subject. I am advised to clam up and let the skin grow over the unclean wound; but the purpose of my writing is to cleanse and purge. What's wrong with trying to gouge out the offending body, to let it be seen instead of hiding it away?

The trouble was, D, that you flattered me; at least in the beginning, you did. 'Write us a novel, Rosamund,' you said. 'I'm sure you could write an excellent one.' (No skin off your nose if it didn't work; no mention of a contract or money — just write us a novel). 'You lucky woman,' I thought, 'being taken seriously by such a famous publisher, a firm that had relics stored away of many an author: the lock of Charlotte Bronte, Byron's sperm in a phial, the consumptive phlegm of Chatterton, and Southey's spittle.'

You wanted to snaffle me up as your prodigy while you played gallantly the nurturer, saviour and Svengali to my Trilby. But, dear D, I'm not your race-horse willing to be trained and coaxed into running the great Booker steeplechase to leap over hurdles and perform literary gymnastics for you.

I'm like a bird, a bird in a cage, if you like (yes, it's not the most brilliant of similes, I must admit) but you see, D, writers *are* like birds. They have a song — their own particular one — which they must sing. Just like mediums who make their minds free and available for something (call it what you will) to come through them. If you clip their wings, or try to modify their song, they atrophy and sometimes even die. So be careful, D, otherwise my song which until recently, has been untampered with, will become clouded and out of tune. You saw what I had to offer, and tried to catch, encapsulate and make it into something marketable not realising that it was as fragile and elusive as a cobweb, it needed to be treated with sensitivity to enable it to blossom.

Why is it, D, that I like you in spite of our differences in opinion? What do you, as the male editor represent for me, the female writer? Who are you? Why do you have such a hypnotic effect? What is it that gets me to respond to you, to acquiesce and accept your demands? With your editing sperm you fertilise my writing egg and an embryo grows. You inject into me something that enables my fruit to gestate and become a child. You may not see it that way, though. Didn't you once refer to Mary Shelley in connection with me; you said that it was you who had given birth to me (a repetition of the distorted Jewish myth) and I was your new writer who, after being created, wouldn't comply and turned into a monster like Frankenstein's.

Somehow, D, you appear to be someone that you so obviously are not; your existence as an editor is purely quixotic; you're there to help people, to nurture promising writers, or so you say. So in my isolation and keenness to succeed I found it easy to lose myself in you (a classic female tendency in a world set up my men) because I had to have someone to write for, someone to pour out all my exuberance and enthusiasm; you, of course, were my nearest port of call; if you thought my writing passed muster, then I was set fair for a good voyage.

You have decried me for being neurotic, fragmented, for not having that cool determination you associate with your male writers. You have no sympathy when I say that there are parts of me neglected because of my life as a writer: the desire for motherhood, for wanting to be both independent and cared for, of wanting both celibacy *and* a lover, of loving women because of their unfailing nearness to what is really important. You do not understand when I say that my writing is taking me away from being my natural self; in other words being a whole woman, a woman who doesn't want to be split in half; expected to be either clever or pretty, but never both; a eunuch — infertile being — or Earth Mother; Virgin Mary or Mary Magdalene. Woman is always seen in polarities; never complexities. She is ironed out into a caricature or seen as a two-dimensional personality purely for man's simplistic comprehension.

I don't know why I come back to you time and time again, D? Maybe it's your manner, D; you're like a sympathetic surgeon or midwife when you stitch up my verse and round off my similes. Such an ingratiating man you are, D. Is it because you're tall, and slim and ever so aloof, D — the classic ex-public school type, D, that gives you authority and credibility with your educated, blasé manner of speaking.

Why didn't you go into politics, D, along with those other smooth Davids? Maybe you should have become someone's think-tank, D, instead of victimising promising authors, D!

The trouble is I don't think you have a clue about writers; you compartmentalise your life; work goes in one box, playing in another and sex in yet another. You fail to understand that for me it is all the same thing: I *am* my work; my work is my libido, my play is my work and libido; I am all bound up in one complicated and incomprehensible ball.

Well, D, what shall I say now? I know what I *want* to say; oh yes I do. You have ruined my story, D, through your crass insensitivity. You have turned it upside down, hoovered it, homogenised and made it as bland and colourless as your boring Home Counties relatives whom I had to talk to for half an hour at the cocktail party you asked me to which was given in some writer's honour; of course, D, I know, and you know also, that I'm not going to write to you (or send off) anything approaching querulousness. You, in your leather-bound haven know that, don't you, D, only too well . . .

Dear D,

I am so sorry I have taken so long to reply to your letter of the 6th. Thank you for sending the proofs of my story. I have read them over, and cannot find anything that I want to add. You wrote that you expected the anthology to be published some time next year when I should receive the second part of my advance. I await happily the date of publication.

Yours sincerely, Rosamund.

ELIZABETH GOWANS

FOOLSCAP

If anything could be blamed from the start, it was probably
Miss Jefferson's bald patch. Ella's classmates had noticed it
right away, from the very first day of the Latin class, and for
a time there had been covert remarks and jokes about it before
Ella herself had ever had a good look. The future tense end-
ings of 'navigo, to steer' gave her the chance, for they hadn't
quite clicked for her and her obtuseness so infuriated Miss
Jefferson that she came marching up the aisle between the
desks, her box pleats going, demanding to see what mon-
strosity in heaven's name Ella had got down in her jotter.
Normally, the teacher examined the exercises unbending,
tracing the words with her forefinger at the end of a long,
stretched arm, her head only slightly inclined. But on this
occasion she thrust her head right down over Ella's page, so
incredible were the mistakes, and began lopping off with her
pencil the offending distortions to the verb.

The famous bald patch came right under Ella's eyes.
There on the crown of the teacher's head, about the size of
a darning ball, it was getting red with her anger and the effort
of leaning over. Ella had seen people who'd lost the odd finger
— folk on farms often had accidents to their hands — and
even a man who'd lost an ear, but this particular instance of
something missing shocked her far more. It was as though
this was the reason for the teacher's driving will to excellence
in her pupils, this unmentionable flaw that she dared them to
notice. In any case, the effect was that Ella's mind stopped
working for a crucial few moments (on Latin) and Miss
Jefferson's angry corrections to 'navigo' were lost on her. She
lurched back to attention as Miss Jefferson was demanding
now did she understand and fixed Ella with a furious look
that Ella in her dismay took to be as much for her impertinent
staring as for her thick-headedness in the Latin. She didn't
dare indicate no better understanding. She had a dreadful
suspicion that Miss Jefferson *knew* and that she walked away
deliberately leaving Ella still at sea, the way open for further
humiliation in front of the class.

It was a class in which Ella was just beginning to feel all right after that awful last year in the qualifying class in the village school. There, she'd had more than her share of attention from the school's girl-bully who led the sneers at any kind of scholarly excellence but extorted, when it suited her, arithmetic answers from class stars. This new school, in a locality nearer Edinburgh, in a matter of weeks had healed much. Ella moved round from subject to subject with the same group of pupils who seemed friendly and clever and, best of all, showed true liking for her. Most of the teachers, too, looked at her kindly, even praised her. At first, she thought this was just the result of having been put in the top class, the one — she'd heard the minister telling her mother — that held 'promise' and was 'a teacher's delight.' The second time she had one of her compositions read out and had a perfect science mark mentioned, Ella began to have an inkling that among her peers she was regarded as having some particular promise that her classmates actually smiled on. She began to be happy as never before. At home, her mother stopped looking at her with worry and was heard telling the minister how Ella these days was 'aye singin' like a lintie.'

One day in November Mr Lamb from the Big House came to see her father about arrangements for the harvest home dance and to ask for names of the guests they were entitled to invite. Ella was struck by the paper Mr Lamb spread on the kitchen table for his lists. The pages were long, lined, a creamy colour, and he had a thick pile of it. He must have noticed her look, for as he left he said 'I'll not be needing all this. Maybe Ella would like some for drawing' and handed her easily half of what he had.

She'd never had such beautiful empty pages in front of her that were not designed for school-work. She put them in the top drawer of the dressing-table where they remained for some time, untouched but giving off in her mind in a queer way an imperceptible sound, like the whisper of the wind in the phone wires when you put your ear against the pole.

That Christmas her present was a green speckled fountain pen and a new bottle of ink. One day, when the snow lay piled in drifts around the house, when her brothers and sister were out with the sledge, her mother baking in the kitchen and her father out on the hill, Ella took the wad of paper out of the drawer and sat down at the dressing-table. It was the only piece of furniture in the house that approximated the height and elbow room of a desk. She looked at herself in the mirror, the hand holding the pen. The angle of the side leaves of the mirror produced multiple images. She adjusted them flat against the wall, giving her more room, and began to write the story. From time to time she'd pause and glance at her reflection.

It was a story about two Cornish children outwitting a pair of sinister smugglers. She contrived each chapter to cover just the two sides of one foolscap, the last sentence being a gem of suspense. She wrote a chapter an evening, positioned thus at the dressing-table, her reflection a kind of friendly companion at whom she'd direct considering looks when searching for the right shape for her sentence. Nobody questioned her disappearing to the bedroom like this after her homework and her share of the chores were done, but she had a sense that what she was doing, if it was not actually an open joke, was received as a bit of amusing play-acting, much like wee Jean's dressing up. It had no harm in it.

As for Ella herself, she found that, having been compelled to start the thing, she had something in her life that was both a pleasure like none other she knew and a tyranny that made sure she did her daily quota even when she thought she might take a little rest from it or, which was dreadful, when she took a peculiar scunner at it as a piece of nonsense, anyway.

When at last the story was finished and she had covered all the fine big pages with her writing, that wasn't enough for her. She wanted to see it now in a form more like a proper book, within the hard covers of a nice, thick notebook — like the ones they used for science, maybe. She ventured to go up after class and ask the science teacher, Mr McCrone, where he got his notebooks. Asked why and what she wanted one for, she explained she had something she wanted to copy up in a notebook like that.

'Something? Valentine verses? Words of famous warblers?'

He was teasing her, she knew, but all the same she was indignant enough to blurt out the real nature of her wish. He was still amused, but the next day he showed her a new, empty science notebook from his store cupboard, saying he would charge her a shilling for it, if her mother was agreeable. So her mother was, after Ella offered to do without a school dinner one day. 'Ye'll dae nae sic thing. Here's your shillin'!'

Her wish to make her story look like a proper book encouraged her to do some drawings to go with certain incidents, her performance in Art being one of her 'promising' traits at school. Now, her evenings were taken up with the copying and sticking in at appropriate places the crayon pictures which she thought quite good herself. Sometimes Mr McCrone would ask her how she was coming along with copying her 'manuscript'. She'd meet his smile with a serious 'fine, thanks.' Close classmates made her promise to let them read it and she airily said they'd get their turn, enjoying her place in their esteem.

One afternoon, Miss Wishart, the English teacher, asked Ella to stay behind after class for a moment. She was a tall lady, always dressed in soft grey or mauve suits with long pleated skirts. She let her jackets swing open showing beautiful Fair Isle jumpers or silk blouses with attached neck ties. Her hair was grey-speckled, coiled round in a bun on her crown. Her voice was young, warm, and she always had an air of being pleasantly surprised. At lunch-time, she and some of the teachers took their meal at an hotel near the school and would be seen strolling back to the gates in a laughing group of which Miss Wishart seemed to be the centre of amusement. Even Miss Jefferson's mouth would twist into a sort of smile and she'd almost swing her handbag.

'I hear,' Miss Wishart said to Ella, putting her elbows on the desk as though getting ready for a chat, 'that you've written a story, Ella. May I be allowed to read it? I'd be *very* interested.'

'All right, Miss. But I've still got a picture and the last chapter to copy.'

'When you've finished, then. Don't forget.'

In this way her renown spread to the staff room. The art teacher commented, surprised, at the illustrations. Someone else suggested the story be sent to Children's Hour on the wireless. Miss Wishart asked permission to let her nieces, great Enid Blyton fans, read the story.

It was during the class spring party that Ella learned that even Miss Jefferson had read her work. The manner and circumstances of her learning this seemed, at the time, quite bizarre — so much so that she was overcome with awkwardness. The incident recurred in her mind, presenting itself like the key to something she might eventually recognise in time.

Ella had almost not gone to the party, having no suitable dress to wear. However, her mother had unearthed a red silk skirt which she'd altered to fit Ella and declared would do fine with her white school blouse. As it was, once the party was in full swing, Ella found that the silk skirt made the

perfect party swish as she was swung from partner to partner
in the reels.

Between dances everyone dropped panting onto benches
round the edge of the polished floor of the gym. One long
bench was placed obliquely across one corner. Behind it were
the chairs for the teachers, as though to emphasise that this
was the pupils' night and *they* were merely spectators. All the
same, most of the teachers got up on the floor for a fling at
some point in the evening.

It was while she was briefly resting on the bench across
the teachers' corner that Ella felt the pluck at her sleeve. She
turned quickly, ready to share the moment of fun with some
friend. Right behind her, leaning forward on her knees, wrists
lolling limply, and with an expression on her face that re-
pelled Ella, was Miss Jefferson. Ella hadn't seen her at the
party till then, as she'd obviously been keeping to herself
there in the corner. She looked so unlike her usual grim self,
the terror of the Latin class. She looked awkward, rather
flushed in the face, like a person blushing. Her black-bead eyes
that could shrivel at the length of a classroom, close up now,
kept turning away and back as she spoke, like someone overcome with shyness but determined to come out with it.

'I've read your story, Ella. I liked it very much.' That was
all.

Totally unready for this untoward, soft, almost abject
approach, and yet sensing that this was Miss Jefferson's bid
to take part in the general warm approval of her, Ella had no
reply but a mystified stare from which she let herself be
wrenched away for the Dashing White Sergeant by a keen
Peter Allen. She must have thrown herself into the dance almost too vigorously for at one point she felt a thud in her
side as a muscle or some other organ in her body protested.
As she steadied herself, taking easier steps, she thought she
caught a glimpse of Miss Jefferson in the teachers' corner
looking at her across the floor with her usual expression of
ire.

Shortly after this, towards the end of May, Ella's father
announced that they were leaving the place, that he was going to a bit in Ayrshire to better himself. The news at school
of Ella's going was received with regret by classmates and
teachers alike, while Ella herself mourned the coming loss
of an environment where she'd never been so happy.

The last week came, the last class being the Latin class.
Miss Jefferson began to speak about the areas of Latin that

she expected the class to have mastered by now. There would be a serious assessment at the end of the term. She wanted *all* of them to begin with a major revision which she would monitor through short weekly tests. She wanted to see *everyone* verb-perfect, vocabulary-perfect, tense-perfect. Was that clear? Were there any questions?

The way she went on about *no one* being excused from this regimen filled Ella with such familiar Latin-anxiety that she had stuck up her hand and explained that she wouldn't be here, they were going away to Ayrshire, before her common sense could warn her just to keep quiet.

Miss Jefferson stared at her for a long moment. The whole class waited. She began her address.

'Ella Yuill.' She made it sound like the ugliest name on earth. 'I . . . am *not* remotely interested in details of *your* personal circumstances. Strange as it may seem to *you*, basking as you do in your own importance, what happens to *you*, where your . . . *family* goes in its wanderings about the country, is not of the least concern to *me* — or anyone else, I should think. Just who do you think you *are? You!* Fancying yourself as an *author*! In—*deed*! You're nothing but a conceited little fool, putting yourself above others, and I say good riddance. *That* . . . is what I've to say to *you*.'

The hideous tirade left her panting, puffed and red with fury. The class was cold-silent.

Ella had begun to shake early on in the blast. By the end she was looking about herself desperately, as for refuge, a place to run to. In the end she lifted the lid of her desk, shutting out the view of the teacher and most of the class, put her head inside and sobbed her heart out.

It was a terrible flood, coming from her mouth, her nose, her eyes, all over the jotters and books. She could not stem it. Peter Allen, who sat behind her, risked a doing by passing her his blotting paper and whispering 'Dinnae you greet for the auld bitch', but his sympathy only added to her misery. The woman's words, like thrown stones, were bad enough. What laid her low was the cruelty and hatred in them, full-grown and frightening.

She was aware while she cried that Miss Jefferson was making efforts to get the lesson going again, asking them to open their books at such and such an exercise. Behind her desk-lid, through the broken sound of her own sobs, Ella could hear her reading the Latin to them in a calm, steady voice, inviting them to ignore the unseemly racket.

Even when she's cried herself dry, Ella left her head inside the desk until the end of the class, dully noting the soaked books and, underneath, the blue corner of the science notebook that contained her story. It was the only thing she took with her at the close of the class, buckling it into her schoolbag and leaving the room without a word to anyone. She felt the concerned looks thrown her way, but she was unapproachable in her hurt. On the school bus she sat wordless and was left alone.

She walked quickly home and hurried into the house to the spot where she'd first begun to be so pleased with herself. Being pleased with yourself was just about a sin, it seemed. She'd heard the phrase often among her own folk. *Ye're surely awfy pleased wi' yersel'*, they'd say, frosty-like.

Ella threw the notebook onto the dressing-table and sat down. She looked at herself in the mirror as she'd done so often while she was at work on her creation. Once again she heard the deadly words of the Latin teacher, her with the frightful missing patch in her head that gave Ella the shivers more than ever now, and she knew she'd never be able to look at herself the same, in the old companionable way. She took hold of the moving side-panels of the mirror and closed them across the centre, shutting away her image of herself.

In the kitchen, in preparation for their flitting, her mother was burning rubbish in the grate. Consigning its fate to someone else's judgment, Ella threw her science notebook onto the pile her mother was sorting through and went outside for a last walk round that familiar place, taking her leave of those particular hedges, those fields of sheep, those burns, and those trees in bud, wondering with some slight measure of consolation about Ayrshire.

ELIZABETH GOWANS

THERE

Isobel always chafed at this bit, thinking fiercely, *I wish he wouldn't come with me. There's no need. I can carry my own case. Why does he do it? I should leave early in the morning, when he hasn't time, instead of waiting for the late train like this.* The whole day was fraught with departure anxiety, anyway, and not enjoyable. But they knew she didn't need to be back till Sunday night, and she couldn't leave earlier in case they'd think she was fed up with being home.

Weekends weren't long enough. Her mother said she was like a square peg in a round hole whenever she went home. She'd glower at the boys' vulgarities, indulged in precisely for her sake, and they'd call her Lady Muck for it. She needed days to settle and to come to know her old place again, when she would get up with grey dawn, put on the fire for her mother, start the porridge and set it on the hob, and be away over to the Ridge to look at the hills, turning her back to the Firth. This was what she came for and missed sorely after weeks of Glasgow. Yet, it seemed the very peacefulness of the hills made her restless. She'd swing round to the bright Firth with its pretty islands and wonder what was wrong with her.

Her homecomings were invariably impulsive. A picture would suddenly spring open in her mind's eye, of the hills, of Fairsden's low slate roof shining in the morning sun, and she'd pack some things into her case and be in the train within the hour. The agitation kept up well through the sooty towns with their back greens and leftover wartime rubble, and only when they got out of the tunnel approaching the Bay, slipping along by the water glinting under the pier, did she feel it beginning to leave her.

The long slow walk over the hill from the station served to get rid of the last of it. It was as though she'd been breathing off the top of her lungs for many weeks. With each crossing of the old lichen-covered fences that constriction gradually went away.

The surprise and pleasure that her unexpected arrival

brought gladdened her at first. She knew they'd been waiting for her to come in the door since her silhouette topped the hill. Daughter and sister, home to see them.

Home. *And where do you belong to?* was what strangers asked strangers on steamers and trains. She belonged to Fairsden, surely, and especially so while she was in Glasgow. Walking over the hill to home, this was ever more clear to her. Walking into your landscape, out there in front, was walking into your own true context, was it not?

Ten minutes into the kitchen and she was aghast at her feelings about her own true context. She could hardly eat for the wish to run away back, to the station, Glasgow University, the Reading Room. She blamed the boys for their provocative jokes, her father for sitting down at the table with dung splashes still on his rolled-up sleeves, and her mother simply for her care-worn look. Worst of all — what brought the feeling to the pitch of nausea — was her guiltiness for ever going away from them and coming back their critic in her heart. *So what did you expect?* she'd jeer at herself, *a Window in Thrums?* The resumption of her childhood tasks — gathering eggs, feeding hens, fetching the cows, seiving milk — gave her some re-entry to the old rhythm and dispelled the nausea.

But something like it seeped back when it grew time for her to go for the train. She'd have preferred to walk back over the hill alone, as she'd come, but her father always came with her to the village road, to carry her case, he said.

They rarely said anything on the way. They both bent their look on the ground. To her mind, it was a clear case of mutual duty being dispatched. He thought he ought to carry the case for her and she was supposed to let him. At the iron gate leading to the paved road:

'Right. There ye are. So. When'll we be seein' ye again, then?'

'Cheerio, dad. Thanks for carrying it. See you all soon.'

'Right. Cheerio, then. I'll away back now. Watch yersel.'

What was there to watch? Tears choking her, she'd stump the rest of the way to the station, not pleased to feel such a bairn about leaving home, and her eighteen, supposedly half-intelligent. Thus she'd rail at herself bitterly.

Once into the train, nearly empty at that time of a Sunday night, the compartment to herself, she could look upon herself more charitably. Regret and apprehension was there, that perhaps she was leaving behind something invaluable that she might lose forever or be cut away from as literally as she was now being carried by the train. So she leaned to the window with her shoulder and scrutinised the fields as they wheeled away. She kept with them until the last of the daylight faded over them and all she could see was her own pensive replica seated in a softly-lit railway carriage.

She looked like a girl in an old picture, not like herself, far nicer than herself. She began to feel more lighthearted and to warm to the lights of the towns. She'd get to the Hall in time for supper and a talk with Janet and Meg. She wondered if they'd started their moral phil. essay. It was a brute this time. *Is Morality Personal?* he'd said, and left them to get on with it. She planned to start on it tomorrow after classes.

Isobel knew she should despise herself for the fact that she loved the ritual of going to classes because of the bright company that moved around her, making the subjects and their lecturers secondary. She liked to see the nonchalant scarves swung over shoulders, their jauntiness with books, and the way they tracked what the lecturer was saying till an innuendo or a pun could be sniffed out and noted with anonymous stamping. She herself didn't feel jaunty (no scarf, fourth-hand books, for a start) but she sat as one of the bright ones, read with them, and could feel infected by what Meg called their 'bold university glee'.

Meg belonged to Isla, was older than her room-mates, and held a decidely amused view of what went on in their seat of enlightenment. She liked to express her age difference through comic primness and had been heard to comment that the most dedicated academic pursuits *she'd* ever seen were conducted not in the Reading Room (though there was a modest amount there) but in the cafes of Byres Road. *And* in Kelvin Grove, *and* in the alley behind the hall, not to mention the front step at the curfew hour, thought Isobel to herself, smiling at her image in the compartment window. One of the Hall rules — indeed, the one most relished by the girls — said that there was to be no 'philandering on the doorstep', and so there was a good deal of it.

Philandering, whispered Isobel, and the memory of her own token participation in that direction brought a little French shrug from her. She made them uneasy, the men she went out with, because her flippancies were too blatant by far. She made fun of the pretence at romance and sometimes this offended. Once, one had called her 'darling' between breath-stopping kisses and she had said back the word, too gruffly, too Dietrich. A pity, that, she thought, but I expect if I told a bloke his kisses were sweeter than wine and he asked me if I meant plonk I'd be offended too.

At the Central Station now, the transition point for hundreds of travellers, she left the train and walked through the milling crowds, glad to be back in the city and finding the yellow haze of lamplit smog alluring, a mysterious element out of which something or someone exciting might emerge. On her return, she moved in the city with new expectation always, although she had no idea what she was waiting for. It was simply a state of inflammation that visited her and made her unaccountably elated for a time. But in the end, nothing happened to match the feeling and she'd gradually come down, the flame reduced to a peep. It was only when this point of light was in danger of utter extinction that she'd flee to Fairsden, and so the cycle went on.

She found Meg in their room, Janet being down at the Reading Room still.

'I thought she'd be out with Rob —Sunday night, after all,' said Isobel, taking off her coat and putting her case up on the wardrobe.

'He has an exam in the morning.'

'They still go out when *she* has one.'

'Oh yes — that being different.'

'Don't see how.'

'Case of personal morality for you — a subject close to the heart at present.'

'What're you reading?'

'Ayer — which is neither heyer nor theyer,' muttered Meg, flipping a page disconsolately and shutting the volume. 'How was your weekend? Are you all swept clean, your inner fires replenished, *la chair moins triste*?'

'Yes, I suppose so.' She avoided answering in the same vein — nothing this time about *la vie simple et pastorale*, shady rills and rivulets, with which they habitually combatted an imaginary romantic in their midst.

The whine of a tram gathering speed carried up the hill from Byres Road. Restless, Isobel paced to the window, and peered out between the drawn curtains.

'Come on for a walk, Meg. Just along Byres Road and back. Or do you want to work?'

'Well, now you've broken what was feeble concentration, anyway, I might as well come with you. Soon be supper as well.'

'Good. We can start fresh in the morning.'

Suddenly exuberant, they belted themselves into their coats and were quickly out on the top doorstep, facing the fog.

'Footsteps in the fog,' murmured Meg. 'Did you ever see that film? Jean Simmons and Stewart Granger. He dies horribly at the end, poisoned by her he tried to poison. Great irony.'

'The swirling mists of the past,' intoned Isobel, as they walked huddled together down towards the street's shop lights. 'Remember Attila the Hun?'

They swung away from each other, laughing loudly, remembering the time last term when they'd been swotting hard to the point of numbness before a history exam and had decided to take a complete break by going to the pictures, any picture. They'd made a point of not asking the usherette what the film was, too. When the title rolled on to the screen Meg whispered 'Oh, *history*.' So prepared were they to be mindlessly entertained and so utterly did *Attila the Hun* strike them as fitting the bill that they laughed inordinately all through and came out weak and subdued.

'Do you ever think how dull we must be, Meg? I mean, look at us, looking forward to a walk along grubby old Byres Road.'

'No. Not dull. Hopeful. After all — Byres Road — it's reality, isn't it? Ordinary, everyday reality, familiar. It must be worth something to us. It's our *dear perpetual place*, you know.'

'Not mine. Mine's ... somewhere else, anyway. Isn't yours Isla?'

Meg walked a few paces without replying and then said with a wry look 'Yes.'

'Wherever I am, Meg, I'm watching for something. It's a strain, in fact, being so — expectant.'

'You see? Hopeful.'

'I'm not sure. Hopefulness should be cheerful.'

'You've got too much of a wandering imagination, that's all.'

'Thanks. Is yours all that harnessed?'

'Absolutely. It's a moral principle with me — now.'

'Well, write that into your essay and maybe I'll think about your point. Look at that frock!'

'Imagine being in *that* — doesn't it look soft!'

'You're not allowed to imagine, remember.'

They went up close to the shop window. Behind the slim wine dress, backing the display, was a long mirror in which they saw themselves reflected. The street behind them looked dark, so that they appeared, expectantly, about to step into the light over the threshold of a door just opened to them.

Meg gave a sigh. 'Ah well, maybe we are dull at that. But next year we'll be in France, thank God.'

'France,' breathed Isobel. 'You know, I have to think of France as a purely fragile possibility or I'd never get any work done in your almighty Here and Now.'

They proceeded along the road arm in arm till they reached the place where it turned into Dumbarton Road, their self-imposed limit. The fog looked worse along this end nearer the river, anyway. And besides, they'd done it — *been out.* 'Out' was where you felt something important was going on all the time when you were not present, reflected Isobel, and it was undoubtedly the place that held the key to absolutely everything. But it moved about — no dear, perpetual place this — and was wherever you were not. Suddenly tired, she said 'Let's go and have supper', and they strode back vigorously.

Two lots of philanderers were standing by the hall gate as they went up the steps. Meg recognised one of them and muttered curfew warnings as she passed, saying she wouldn't be held responsible if 'that girl' was late in, to which a masculine voice muttered back that she wouldn't be *held.* They went in laughing.

Isobel finished the day by reading two chapters of *Bovary*, a required text she had little liking for so far. When she turned off the light she stayed leaning on her elbow for a moment, peering at the sudden darkness in the room until her eyes got used to it and it was relieved somewhat by the infiltration of the last street lights. A dark patch showed up on the mirror. It was a postcard print of *L'Angélus* which she kept stuck in the frame. She remembered dusk at Fairsden as she lay down on the pillow.

The hurry-bell for eight o'clock classes was ringing urgently when she woke up. Grateful not to have one of these this term, she got up and went to the window. A white day again. Like an empty page. Was it Mallarmé who felt both the invitation and the granite resistance of the blank page? She ought to know that.

Through the moral phil. lecture and the following hour on Baudelaire Isobel devoutly took notes behind her hair that brushed the notebook as she leaned over it. There was to be no jocularity this Monday morning. Below the edge of the desk she could see the legs of pressed grey flannels seated on her right. He wasn't writing anything down. Some never needed to, it seemed.

Suddenly he leaned down and put aside the fall of her hair with the back of his hand. 'Give us a keek! What was that last bit? *Tout n'est qu'ordre et* ... What's that last word?'

'*Beauté*,' she said, looking up. It was the one she and Meg had christened, with obvious tribute, Adonis. He had fair curls all over his entirely beautiful head.

'*Beauté?*' he quizzed her, looking from her notes to her face, still holding up her hair matter-of-factly.

'*Beauté*,' she reassured him and began to smile. He was Glaswegian enough. He repeated '*ordre et beauté*' once more, nodding, and then removed his hand and said 'Curtain!'

She straightened up and closed the notebook, indicating the podium.

'*La classe est finie,*' she whispered. He repeated '*finie*' and sighed pointedly over the word for her.

Along with the rest of the class they stood up to file out, waiting in turn to get to the aisle. She was aware of him whistling softly through his teeth behind her.

Then '*Mademoiselle, ecoutez-moi* ... ' just audible. But she wasn't ready to play yet.

He became Chinese. 'Excuse, pleese. Why you hide behind hayuh?'

She turned laughing. 'Away from fiendish nosy folk, of course.'

'Hm. Is velly nice hayuh. I watch.'

They shuffled nearer the aisle, his shuffle bringing him right up against her shoulders. She waited for his next step, but he was whistling under his breath. Then as they reached the aisle and were about to separate in mingling with the crowd, he said suddenly into her ear 'See you at the Reading Room tonight.' She looked up to find him giving a wink and a smile, quoting '*Là, tout n'est qu'ordre et beauté,* don't you know.'

She was smiling too as she left the lecture hall. The tempo of the day had quickened.

Later on, right after dinner at the Hall, she gathered together books, notes and references she'd need for a good three-hour stint in the Reading Room to work on the essay.

The best part of the study ritual was getting the pile of materials together. One felt purposeful running downstairs carrying them. And the five-minute walk to the Reading Room held the exhilaration that accompanies a pure resolve.

It was another foggy evening, with small rain in it. Isobel clutched her books close to her as she hurried out, hurried forward into the fog, breathing shortly with expectation.

Close to the high iron gate leading to the Reading Room steps a figure in a raincoat emerged from the gloom in front of her, approaching up the hill. She was about to turn in at the gate when he spoke.

'Excuse me. Could you tell me the way to Kelvin Hall?'

'Kelvin? Oh, yes. Let's see. You need to go back down the hill and the quickest way is to go through Kelvin Grove. It's just the other side, that crescent you'll see, quite a wide curve it has.'

'Oh, yes.'

'Are you going to go there?'

'Yes. My father was up to see it last week and he told me it was very good. Worth seeing.'

'Oh. I've some friends there — they like it.'

'Oh?'

He was looking at her in silence. She suddenly saw him. The raincoat was wet, a drab gabardine. He wore glasses that were wet with the rain, as was his hair, deep yellow curls. He had boots on, and it was the boots that sent her mind backtracking, hearing afresh what he had been saying to her. She saw, with a queer pang, her mistake.

'Wait,' she said. 'I thought you were looking for one of the students' residential halls here. The name's the same. But you're wanting the Agricultural Show, aren't you?'

'Aye, that's right — the Kelvin Hall.'

'I'm sorry. It's actually a lot easier. Just down the hill there, turn right and walk straight out to the first big road. It'll be facing you. You'll know it.'

'Right. Thanks very much.'

His hands were stuffed into the raincoat pockets so that he leaned slightly forward. The rain on his glasses had gleamed in the lamplight so that she hadn't seen his eyes properly. As he turned to go he kept his look on her still for a moment. The light altered and she saw that his eyes were puzzled and vaguely apologetic, as though he were the one sorry for the mistake and sorry that he wasn't what she had thought.

Isobel turned slowly to go in at the gate again, then turned slowly to look after the boy. She could hear the echoing clump of his boots still. They had probably tramped over fields to get to a train to bring him to Glasgow. He could have been kin and she'd not recognised him. She wished she'd talked to him now, asked where he belonged to, what his place was called, told him where she belonged.

Presently, aware of the books in her arms and the gates in front of her, she was near tears. She had a sense of imbalance, of displacement. Any heart for work now drained away.

She turned from the gates and retraced her way back to the Hall and her room. Her copy of *Bovary* lay on the bed. It made her recall what Meg had said last night. 'Thank God we'll be in France next year.'

The thought of France at this moment eased her. She'd like to be sent somewhere in Anjou. *La douceur angevine.* Or perhaps Savoie. *Etoile des neiges.* Wasn't the light supposed to be special somewhere in France? Or was that Greece? She must watch for that special light. Watch yourself, he'd said. Not yet. She touched with her forefinger the postcard stuck in the mirror and whispered the soothing words over:

> *Là, tout n'est qu'ordre et beauté,*
> *Luxe, calme et volupté.*

IAIN CRICHTON SMITH

ROMAN POEMS

THE INVASION

'When will the Gauls invade us?'
I hear the city whine.
'They're bayonetting children
along the Apennine.'
Time for the newscasters, I would say,
to scribble their memoirs
and recall our ageing generals
to fight in earlier wars.

Our gardens in uneasy calm
wait for the boots to stride
over elitist blossoms
to the works of art inside
hung by illiterate millionaires
as safer than our coin,
insurance from the crippled men
who died of cheap red wine.

No statement anyone can make
but breeds its opposite now.
The gods have left us howling.
The fabled Golden Bough
shines on young killers in the wood
tracking the infirm king
who's brought to bay by end of day
and dies within their ring.

Before the riders ever towered
above the gates of Rome
our nerves had snapped like bowstrings
we'd fashioned our own doom
in poems, paintings, politics.
The Left struck at the heart,
and joined with Rightist ignorance
in their contempt for art.

No longer shall our buildings stand.
Without, within, we quake,
we went to sleep in careless dreams,
in nightmares we awake,
and when the shadowy conquerors
guzzle at thinning shelves
we recognized them from our sleep
as portraits of ourselves,

the violent Ids that we have seen
from pillows calm and white
projected on demonic screens
in the long boring night
arising to devour us now
in reality gone wrong,
as Tiber's waters flood the world
and raise their nightmare song,

disoriented, sharp and pure,
with the amoral child's
wish to possess his mother,
destroy his father's shields,
and live forever by itself
in the waste it calls its own,
the total freedom of its wish
and the smashed toy of Rome.

MARCUS AURELIUS SPEAKS

I have to leave insomniac Rome
to guard the borders, so
farewell verse and farewell prose,
and farewell, spare philosophy,
I go to the sleet and snow.

Patricians and plebs have fought.
Many-talented Caesar struck
At Pompey's men, 'Strike at the vein.
It will cause the greatest panic to
open them like a book.'

And crazed Augustus cried all night,
'My legions, where are they?
O give me back again those men.'
And the swan-breasted blue-eyed Gauls
rushed on us day by day.

Nero and Caligula,
insane dictators both,
saw seething Rome as a boring home.
What pathological disease
was present at Rome's birth?

And so we build our creaking walls
to keep the madmen in,
and to keep out those without doubt
who crave the marble and the trees
even Hannibal couldn't win,

who learned one day that the mile of ground
on which his camp was built
had just been bought by a Roman fraught
with such an immense confidence
it made the great man wilt.

And I march out with legionnaires
to defend a dying day.
('Who hasn't seen great Rome's demesne
has never seen the sun itself,'
or so they used to say.)

I shall post myself in my cold tent,
last Stoic of my kind,
and watch the rain fall over Spain
and steadily and malignantly
watch to the very end,

voyeur of our obscenity,
and the future's confident waves.
Show them the flag. Far back there dig
the gnomes who are undermining
their defenders' sleety graves.

The Carthaginian women wove
bowstrings from their hair.
But Carthage burned and Scipio turned
on his playful horse away from the light
and omens of that air.

I see the words DELENDA EST
as now applied to Rome
as now I gaze at the piercing stars
which know no walls or borders
of our proud imperium.

Farewell, you sordid marketplace,
and forums of quick lies,
and gladiators and realtors,
The Theatre of Cruelty,
and the silence of the wise.

I'll watch for you at the world's end
in my doubtful armour till
the nameless cohorts take your forts
and the unmarbled mishmash turn
on the unforgiving wheel.

I'll watch for the simplicities
Of which Cato used to speak
and the herbs so common and acerb
on which were nursed the principles
where armies used to break,

and heroes like our Mucius
who roasted his own hand
to show how Rome had a firm bone
which like the rocky Apennines
was central to our land.

So, as the border's lost in snow,
I shall watch a new day rise
and on this field with fading shield
be dazzled by the foreigners
with the familiar eyes

of Romans out of story books
huge giants of past days
who in this present use the crescent
hooked weapons of the harvest time
that topples from their gaze.

THE ATOMS

The Lares and Penates by
Lucretius are hurled
out of the marble villas
to the sparse atomic world
where Neptune, Mars, and Venus
diminish on the screen
of the Roman nox with its safety locks
and the human light between.

The dead will not return again
to the forum of vast Rome
nor ever stroll at evening
by the marble of their home,
but speechless, ruined and extinct,
seethe in the Roman mould
while sunny clocks and rugged rocks
tick through the heat and cold.

Their ghosts will not revisit
the tragic or comic plays,
nor above stained arenas
watch bloody panthers graze
on gladiators with short swords
while the bored emperors lean
to crack a joke to the black cloak
Death sports behind the scenes.

The atoms clash and coalesce
beyond the Roman roads.
Their minimal shields and fields of force
are stronger than the gods.
Eerie and grave in the vast wastes
where legions never go
they break, reform, attack and storm
the tents of Scipio.

Inventive, accidental,
the primitive desires
which feed the will of Caesar
and banked Cleopatra's fires,
power Cicero's orations
and the envy of the Gauls
and make the plebs howl like the tribes
which beset our city walls,

and make both Death and Love the brief
spasms of mindless will.
For there's no Hades for proud ghosts
to stroll on asphodel
but only the huge silence
which falls when Rome will fade
from a single soul — and the state will roll
to irreversible shade.

I. McFADYEN

BIRDSNESTS

today
I walked

looked for
birdsnests and
poems

once
I looked
only for
birdsnests

poems were
everywhere

GEESE

That I choose you or
you choose me to
make our lives together is
a lie:

whatever binds us
is whatever holds this
arrow of grey geese
straight in the sky.

DODO

Others must
fly — a
vulgar accomplishment, necessitating the
expenditure of
unthinkable quantities of valuable
energy, which our
ancestors in their
venerable wisdom
disdained. For what is
air but
nothingness, the domain of
fools of
albatrosses?
Warmth, comfort, ease and food in
plenty: these are
fruits of the
solid ground. We are
masters of the
Earth.
Strong legs and beaks, not
wings, have made it so, and
none dares
challenge us.
Flight! We have
eliminated even
haste. Only the
encumbrance of these
wings maintains us in
humility — reminds us we are
birds like other creatures. We
thank Providence for our
supremacy.
Heretical flying
fools may say there's
life beyond
this island, we are not
creation's crown. We
pay no heed. There is
no life beyond that
we can see. Where are these
other beings?
Let them appear!

SCORPIONS

Scorpions are
meek. Disturbed, they
scuttle under stones. If
pushed, tails raised, they
dart and threaten — and
cornered, they
defend with deadly venom. (Some can
fell a horse.) But mostly, they are
meek. Corners, crevices,
deserts, dark holes — such
poor places are
all they ask.
Stone is their
element. Time has
etched them on rock
older than reptile, mammal, bird. Their
eight-legged line is a
long one. They are
survivors. They go months without
water, fast forty days (plus)
all the time, can
walk out of
iceblocks or
ovens. They are
modest about such
miracles. But (and this is the
sting in the tale) they and
they alone can
amble unharmed through
poisoned deserts men make with
atomic bombs. So
regard them with
respect. They will
probably
inherit the Earth.

THOMAS F. DOCHERTY

EDINBURGH SCHOOLGIRL

He'd been stupid to come. These public-school creeps always annoyed him and when he was annoyed he fenced badly. And their stuck-up girlfriends, snobbish bitches, with their la-di-da east coast accents.

He continued to put on his gear. Over the plastron protecting his right side, the light nylon jacket. He noted with disapproval its off-white tint. Bought in a closing-down sale in Arnold's, it had been a half-price bargain, but still, compared with the snowy-white gear of other competitors . . . He shrugged and fed the body-wire for his electric foil down the inside of his right-hand sleeve, till it dangled clear of his hand by several inches. He clipped the other end of the wire loosely to the buckle of his jacket at the back. Next he put on the over-plastron, the gold-lamé sleeveless jacket which was needed when fencing with electric foils, to register any valid hits which his opponent might make on his target.

He got up, a little awkwardly, lifted his sports bag and foil-case, and went into the Competition Hall. The place was quite full and already the heat was noticeable. The first rivulet of sweat traced its way down his ribs. He went over to the check-in table, gave his name and showed his Association Card, then walked over to the side of one of the pistes, where there were only two or three other competitors. He dumped his bag on the floor and opened the foil-case. Inside, there were the two electric fencing foils. He'd checked them several times the night before; he knew they were in good working order, but there was always that niggling little worry — would one of them be acting up today . . .

He looked around the hall. There was Morrison, over under the clock. Good fencer. He'd met him a couple of times down in England. And McKay beside him. Aye, and there was the big Spanish lad . . . what was his name . . . mean big sod, and a left-hander as well. Hope he wasn't in the first pool. Then he saw him — Campbell, Alistair Campbell, the Great White Hope of the East. A tall blond boy, handsome enough to make you puke, with the usual bunch of daft lassies

clustered round him. He stared over at Campbell, remembering the first time he'd fought him. A big fly man, full of the
clever wee tricks to put you off your game, but a top-class
fencer for all that. Campbell was telling a joke. That was obvious the way the girls were tittering in anticipation of the
punch-line. When it came, they fell about. He noticed one of
them particularly, shoulder-length blond hair, and a wide
mouth, opened in a scream of laughter. Silly bitch, he thought.
But a nice looking silly bitch, said the wee jeering voice in his
head. You wouldn't mind that hanging on your arm, laughing
at your jokes. Aye, and you wouldn't mind looking like
Campbell, either. He turned away irritably, and picked up his
fencing mask. Three or four small dents in it, but nothing
serious enough to disqualify it.

At that moment the microphone over at the check-in
table gave a preliminary squeal. The uproar of conversations
died away gradually and a voice began to call out the names
of the contestants for the first pools. He listened attentively.
Nobody he knew in his pool. Fine. He glanced over at Campbell and met the other's eyes. They looked at each other
across the hall, then Campbell turned and said something to
the girl. Both of them looked over at him.

'You ready?' a voice behind him asked.

He turned and looked at the questioner.

'Aye,' he said, 'any time.'

The other nodded and pointed to a group waiting at the
side of a piste two up from him. He walked over and joined
them. They looked at him incuriously and went on with their
conversations. A tall, tweedy man called for silence and read
out the order in which the contestants would fence. He was
on second. He looked over at his opponent-to-be. A lanky,
sandy-haired boy he'd never seen before. Fair enough, he
thought, as he saw the boy was wearing his protective glove
on his right hand, at least it wasn't a southpaw for starters.

The first bout was pretty grim, with the two fencers
hacking and flailing about like rank beginners. He watched in
disgust, then thought, careful, there had been that clown at
Paisley who had seemed so slow and clumsy, but had scored
three hits on him before he'd got the measure of him. Careful, take nobody at face value. Fence them all as cautiously as
you would the very best till you knew their worth then take
them out as fast as you can. Save yourself for the big boys in
the semis and finals.

Now it was his turn. Behind him, on the floor, was the

heavy spool containing the spring-loaded cable into which each fencer had to plug his personal body-wire, in order that hits made on their bodies would light up the indicator lamps for the spectators to follow the play. The cable came and went with the movement of the fencers. One of the waiting contestants stepped forward and offered to help him wire-up.

'No,' he said, 'I'll do it myself,' then conscious of the ungracious tone of his statement, he added, 'But thanks, anyway.'

The preliminaries over, he lifted his mask, ensured that the body-wire socket was firmly connected to his foil, and saluted his opponent in his usual punctilious manner. Slob, he thought, as the other sketched the briefest acknowledgement of his salute, do they no' teach you manners in your Salle? He put on the mask.

He adopted the classic fighting stance which was now second nature to him: feet about ten inches apart, heels at right angles, knees deeply flexed, left arm up behind him, sword-arm bent, with elbow at waist-level, the weapon at an angle of 45 degrees to the floor, point level with his eye, towards his opponent. He waited a moment, then extended his arm, step, step, into the lunge and hit his opponent squarely in the middle of the chest. The light on the indicator behind the other flashed the valid hit. He shook his head slightly in disbelief. Sandy-hair had scarcely stepped back and his defensive parry had been so slow as to be a joke. Fine, if he's that poor, let's try the same move again. The bout lasted a further two minutes — enough to score the remaining four hits to give him a five-nothing victory. He shook hands with Sandy-hair and disconnected his body-wire. The rest of the fights in that pool were scarcely more demanding and he felt vaguely cheated. This wasn't what he needed to get him into the mood to beat Morrison or Campbell. Incidentally, how was Campbell doing? He looked over at the piste where the blond boy was just finishing a bout against one of the other public-school types. The indicators showed that Campbell was leading 4-2. Even as he watched, Campbell finished the bout with a vicious lunge, and the lights flashed up the final 5-2. The blonde who had been cheering Campbell on throughout the bout, screamed with glee and hugged her hero as he walked off the piste.

And then a most curious thing happened. The girl turned and looked across at him. He stood still, returning her steady look. In repose now, her face was stunningly beautiful, the wide mouth closed in a slight smile, the vivid blue eyes gazing into his. For about three or four seconds those eyes looked steadily at him, then the girl turned back to Campbell.

His legs felt weak. They really did. It was unbelievable. A silly lassie in a posh blazer from some snob Edinburgh school had looked at him and he felt as if he'd been punched in the gut. Come on, he told himself, get a grip, man. But the wee jeering voice lacked conviction. She'd looked at him, and something . . . something magic had happened. With mounting excitement, he looked over at Campbell. Your girl smiled at me, big man. I'll take you today, pal, I'll take you.

In the second pool it was as if he were fencing on air. Between bouts he stole glances over at Campbell's piste. The girl was still there, along with some others, and they yelled and cheered as Campbell played. Once the girl looked over at him, with that same steady gaze, and he felt the blood hot in his face.

His last bout in the semi-finals was against a left-hander, but he couldn't do a thing wrong. The other man was good, he conceded, and his defence was a tight one, but he knew he had the beating of him. The bout wore on, neither fencer giving anything away, one as cunning as the other. He was aware that the bouts in the other pools had finished and that a rapidly growing number of spectators had gathered round them. And she was one of them. She'd left Campbell sitting holding court at the far end of the hall and she was watching . . . watching him. Fine, he thought, I'll give you something to watch, then.

Coldly he settled down to play his man. Lean to the right, keep the point out to the right and step round into him. Aim for the ribs below his guard, below the left elbow and — and Southpaw nearly had him with a lunge, drawing his lateral parry into quarte, then a feint and the attack was completed into his opened line of sixte. His frantic back-hand parry barely blocked the other's blade, and into you! he exulted, glancing his blade off his opponent's and into the latter's unguarded chest. The lights flashed up the valid hit.

He was remotely aware of an unusually tense silence around the piste. The spectators seemed to press inwards, intent on the two white-clad figures. Aye, he thought, get a good look at the lad that's going to cuff your man Campbell today. And she was watching. But Southpaw was good. A cool one, accustomed to winning and not worried at all that the first hit was against him. A relaxed guard that drifted carelessly across the body, too carelessly, inviting an attack which would be parried and maybe followed by a clever wee sequence of counterparries, counter-ripostes and that's one in the bag for lefty — and the fleche took him nicely in the lower ribs with stinging force. Anger at the pain surged up in him, but he fought it down. You lost when you got angry. Next round, three seconds into it, he fleched, without even thinking about it and took Southpaw completely by surprise. For him! Sweat was bathing his ribs now, smarting where the other's blade had hit him previously. I'll have a stotter of a bruise there tomorrow, he thought, and saw her smiling at him, not mockingly, but aye, admiringly! His discomfort vanished as if wiped away and he was unbeatable. It wasn't easy, he'd be the first to admit it, but he fought Lefty to a 5-4 finish, and the crowd was cheering him.

At the end of the bout, he took off his mask and shook hands with his opponent. Southpaw smiled, unruffled by defeat, though his face was crimson with effort and heat. A brief, comradely gesture of the hand, and Southpaw turned and pushed his way through the spectators.

He turned to unplug his body-wire from the cable, but she was there, her hands already unfastening the connection. She looked at him, her face expressionless and said, 'You're from Glasgow, aren't you?'

He nodded, unable to speak — the heat and exertion had parched his throat he told himself — and she handed him the body-wire.

'You're good,' she said and turned away to walk back to King Campbell and his court.

For a few seconds he stood there, his face burning, hearing again those . . . *silver* tones . . . aye, that was the word.

Hernandez had not made it to the finals. Hard luck, he thought, but he was relieved. His own name was announced, then Morrison's, two others and there it was — Campbell's.

You're dead, pal, he thought with absolute conviction. You're dead, and I'm going to bury you.

They were the last, he and Campbell. The other fights had been hard, but with the way he felt knowing she was watching, they had really honed him to a perfection which was going to destroy Campbell.

He stood waiting, enjoying the tenseness around him, the almost tangible concern that pulsed from the Campbell supporters. Aye, you're right to worry, he jeered within himself, I'm going to beat your Alistair and that shield's going back with me to Glasgow, tonight.

The President asked the ritual question:

'Are you ready?'

'Ready,' he replied.

'Ready,' said Campbell.

'Fence!' said the President.

They advanced to meet each other, two faceless figures their heads encased in the blank anonymity of their masks. Around them silence, like a wall, cutting them off from the real world. But their reality was this piste, the cold clinical glare of the lights, the swish of their feet on the slight yieldingness of the metallic strip, the click and scrape of blade probing blade. Fine, he thought, I've never fenced better, never felt this good. Cold, unflustered, keyed up to the utmost, the ultimate confrontation.

And now the score stood at 4-4. The deciding hit was going to be his, of that there was no doubt. She was there, silent, motionless; she had not made a sound nor a move since the start of this bout.

He moved towards Campbell. The other moved back, keeping the distance constant between them. He knew now the move he must make, the move that would give him the shield, the title, the satisfaction of proving himself superior to them all.

He began his move, his mind as cold and analytical as a Grand Master's, knowing that Campbell was a dead man, knowing that he had him now and . . .

'Get the bastard, Alistair!' the silver tones rang out in the dead silence, and for a tenth of a second he hung there, disbelieving, and Campbell's point took him squarely in the chest.

Uproar. The President's voice calling for order. Campbell standing there, enigmatic. Some official or other protesting about the scandalous behaviour of spectators, and himself knowing fine well it wouldn't change a thing. There was no disputing it. Campbell had scored the last hit and Campbell had won. End of story. The shield would stay in Edinburgh after all. He took off his mask, shook hands with Campbell and looked at the blond girl. She returned his look and smiled. Bitch, he thought, but there was no real anger in him. He nodded once to Campbell and turned away. He caught sight of the clock under which Morrison had stood. Eight-fifteen. If he hurried, he would make the nine o'clock train to Glasgow.

IAN RANKIN

COLONY

He spent much of that long, hot summer in the garden at the back of the house, watching a colony of ants keep busy between the cracks in the crazy paving. The paving-stones made up a bizarre sort of chess-board, and all manner of insects — but especially ants — would rear up from the grass-tufted gaps between the slabs, scurrying across the hot surface of the stone before disappearing again.

There was nothing else to be done in the town, one of Scotland's very own creations of the 1960s, the cement dream of some distant architect. Boy and town had grown together in mutual antipathy, and now there was nothing to be done. Besides, he felt held to the house by an irresistible force. He wanted to know what would happen.

He found that he could agitate the insects by jumping up and down on the spot, sending earthquakes quivering through their minds and their bodies, causing them to spin in alarmed circles beneath the sunshine and his larger shadow, well out of their domain. In this way, he knew, he could master them, but he preferred to sit in cooler silence on a chair, head between his knees, examining the tireless work of the colony. He was a quiet child by nature, and nobody seemed to mind his silence, his isolation, and his preoccupation.

His mother stayed indoors most of the time, humming melodies to herself as she cleaned, washed, ironed, cooked, tidied and made telephone calls. If he came into the house for some squash, she would put down the telephone and ask him if he were not too hot, his face being red.

Her face would be red, too, but not from watching the colony.

His sister had a summer job at a factory, picking defective peas and tiny pieces of stone from a constantly moving conveyor-belt. She said that she felt dizzy sometimes, stupefied by the endless procession of green. She wouldn't eat another pea as long as she lived. The job gave his sister the money she needed in order to stay out of the house for increasingly long evenings and weekends. He did not mind his invisible sister, who was four years older than him. Next year, just as he was entering her school, she would be leaving it to find a job, thus retaining her invisibility. He had asked her once if she would marry.

'Never,' she said. 'Never on your life. I'll get a job and I'll do very well on my own, thanks very much.' She threw back her hair. It was long and black, falling in fine strands across her shoulders. 'Look at mum and dad,' she said. 'If that's what they call marriage . . . '

His face turned red. They had never talked about it before. He felt a little closer to his sister then, and told her a long story about a boy who picked on him at school. He elaborated as much as he could, because he could see that he had her attention. He had never had her attention before. And all the while he was thinking about what she had said, about their mum and dad, about it. She had mentioned it, so it must be true then. Of course it was true.

The ants worked well together. There seemed to be a system behind everything they did. When he blocked the entrance to one of their tunnels with a large crumb of bread, they soon formed themselves into a sort of tug-of-war team, holding onto the bread with their pincers and pulling hard. It took them an hour to dislodge the obstacle, and having done so they did not stop to rest, but went off again to hunt and gather whatever was necessary to the colony.

'I'm just going off to the shops. Do you want to come?'

'No.'

He would sit beneath the kitchen window and listen to his mother on the telephone. She spoke very quietly, giggling occasionally. The telephone bill would be enormous. He calculated the cost of a daytime call such as his mother made. He chewed on a piece of yellow grass and watched two of his ants attacking another insect who for some reason had become their enemy.

Once, he had answered the telephone and a man's voice had asked to speak to Mrs Renshaw. The man had sounded polite and official, but when his mother had thought him outside, her voice had become weightless, like a schoolgirl's, and she had giggled. All that afternoon she hummed brisker melodies to herself, rubbing her son's hair whenever he strayed too close to her.

His father worked in an office and carried a briefcase

home with him at night. He worked in the evening at the kitchen-table, opening the briefcase and carefully lifting out documents, wiping the surface of the table before putting them down on it. He rolled a pen in his mouth and stared at the sink, the cooker, the washing-machine, as though ticking these things off on a list in his mind. Then he would stand at the living-room door, watching his wife as she watched the television, running his hand over his head as though he had been swimming. His hair was thin. He picked an occasional strand from his shoulder and examined it, his eyes full of something like accusation.

One day his father came home a little too early from work, and when the telephone rang in the kitchen he answered it very quickly, talking loudly into the mouthpiece. His son watched from the doorway, a book in his hands. Ants, it seemed, inject an acid into their enemies so that they die quickly but in great pain. For ants, even death had its system.

When she remembered, his mother brought him books about insects from the town's well-stocked library. He didn't read these books really, preferring to look at the illustrations. He found that the coldly human words destroyed his own ideas about the ants, and he much preferred his own ideas to those of the people who wrote the books. He looked at the pictures with the books lying on the ground and his head between his knees on the chair. Sometimes an ant would wander onto the page and circle across the paper without recognising itself there, magnified a thousand times.

The back of his neck became burnt, but he did nothing about it. He liked to lie in bed at night with his hand grazing the hot skin. He lay curled up in a ball, the bedcovers kicked away from him, holding his breath and hoping that his sister would not come home too late, that his father would not shout at her, that his father and mother would not argue in the living-room. Whenever they did, he rubbed hard at his neck, feeling the one pain replace the other, wishing that he could speed up time so that his father might leave for work all the sooner. His mother seemed so much happier during the day, though her humming had taken on a slightly broken edge, as though she had forgotten all the songs that once she had taught him. He wanted to make her come out into the garden, where she would be safe and would see things differently, but he knew that his ants seemed too small to her to be of interest.

But ants were strong, and organized, and busy. He felt tired from watching their activity. If one ant happened to pause while crossing a flagstone, he would wonder if it were contemplating the reasons behind all this activity.

He showed his sister some of the routes along which the insects operated.

'Do you see that little hole? Well, just watch it. They come in and out of there. And look here, between the cracks. Do you see? They are moving two-deep down there, one line walking over the backs of the other. How do you fancy being on the bottom line?'

'Yuck. They're not a pretty sight, are they. I thought the peas were bad enough. Is this what you do with yourself then? Sit and watch ants all day?'

'Yes. It keeps me out of the house.'

His sister looked at him. Her eyes were dark with scrapings of mascara, and something deeper. She made to rub his head, but he ducked, coming up bobbing and weaving. She laughed.

'I've got to go now,' she said. She gestured towards the flagstones. 'Goodbye, ants,' she said.

At the very end of the summer, when the wind was beginning to colour the Fife skies grey instead of blue, his sister did not come home for three days running. She had telephoned home on the second night, and his father had spoken to her while his mother listened closely at the receiver.

'She wants to speak to you,' his father said, pushing the telephone towards him.

His parents watched while he took the receiver nervously. 'Hello?'

'Hello there,' she said. Her voice was a little higher than usual, a little more breathy. She was swallowing hard. 'How are the ants?' she asked.

'They're okay,' he said.

Later, there was an argument between his parents. He walked out into the garden so as to be far away from the shouting. Those shouts churned his stomach. He placed his ear to one of the paving-slabs and tried to hear the ants moving, one line across the body of the other line, far beneath him. The telephone rang in the kitchen and there was a rush to answer it. His mother won, but then his father took the receiver and shouted into it while his mother railed against him. The argument was moved into the kitchen for a while

after that, and then there was silence, except for quiet footsteps up the stairs of the house. Finally, his father opened the
kitchen door and stepped outside.

'Oh, there you are, Tim. I've been looking for you, What
are you up to?'

'I'm just . . . nothing.' His face was red, while his father's
was incredibly white, white as the hands of his great-grandmother, who lived in a nursing-home in Edinburgh and who
could not hear and could not see. He wanted to tell his father
about the ants, but he could see that his father would not
want to listen just now.

'This garden's in a bit of a state, isn't it? Weeds all along
the path and everything.' His father began to pace the garden,
pretending to inspect the bushes and the grass. 'Your mum's
been going on about it for ages now. Well, I'll clear it up tomorrow. Will you give me a hand, or do I have to break a
back by myself?'

'But tomorrow's only Thursday. You work on Thursday.'

His father crouched in front of him. Tim, despite himself,
looked at the thinning hair.

'I'm going to take a few days off, Tim. Maybe a week
even. We'll tidy up the garden, and we could even go fishing.
Would you like that?'

Embarrassed by the milkiness of his father's eyes, Tim
nodded.

'Good,' his father said, laying a hand on his son's tight,
hot neck. 'Things haven't been too good recently, have they?
But your mum and me are going to straighten everything out.
You'll see.'

When his father had gone back into the house, Tim stared
for a long time at the flagstones. Then he began to jump up
and down on the spot, bringing himself down onto the cement
with all the power he had. An ant poked its head out of one
of the entrances, looking ready to complain about the disturb-
ance. Tim crouched beside the tiny figure. Tomorrow he
would help his father in the garden and tell him all about the
colony.

His mother, however, asked him to go shopping with her
in the town. She promised him a present of a new football
strip for school if he went. He put on his shoes and jacket,
and watched his father through the kitchen window as he
paced the garden, examining what needed to be done.

His mother allowed him to go to the record-shops alone,

giving him some money. She seemed nervous, her face red at the cheekbones. They met later outside a restaurant. She did not want to go in, though he had offered to buy her a cup of coffee with her change. She said that she had already had a cup of coffee with a friend. Well, not really a friend. Just someone she had worked with once. They had to go home now. She had the evening meal to cook, and his sister would be coming home tonight. She had forgotten all about buying him a football strip. He asked her if anything was wrong. She looked at him strangely, then smiled.

'Of course not,' she said, and squeezed his shoulder.

When they arrived home, his father was washing his hands in the kitchen. He was wearing an old overall, and his head and chest were dusty with a light grey powder. Strands of hair sweated on his brow.

'There were no phone calls,' he said, seeming quite pleased with himself.

'No. I didn't think there would be.'

His mother began to put some things into the refrigerator and take out others.

'And I've started to that garden,' said his father. 'It'll look fine once I've cleared away the cement.'

He ran past his father and stepped outside. Each and every crack between the paving stones had been newly filled with wet cement.

'That should put a stop to the weeds,' said his father from the kitchen door. 'At least for a time. Your mother was always complaining about those weeds, and quite rightly too. But that'll sort them. You should have stayed at home, Tim. You could have helped. Watch you don't get dirty.'

He walked over the concrete slabs. There were no gaps, no holes. It was a meticulous piece of work. No insects scurried across the stones, even when he jumped up and down on the spot. Everything was as still as a cemetery. A small pile of unused grey cement lay beneath the kitchen window. There was a wheelbarrow, too, with a shovel and a small trowel lying in it. Inside the kitchen window, his mother and father were embracing.

He looked away and saw that a line of cement between two stones near the barrow had a small bubble in it. On his knees, he put his head close to the bubble and pricked it with his finger. It burst slowly, leaving a tiny gap in the cement. He did not have to wait long. Soon the first ant was examining, a little shakily, this new entrance. It signalled to the rest of the colony that all was well, and they began to follow it upwards. He looked for more bubbles and found lots of them, pricking them too. Soon the ants were circling across the stones again, dancing in the fresh air and the light. He sat and watched them, smiling to himself and touching his neck. His sister sat down beside him and he told her his secret.

'I wonder if I should tell mum and dad about it?'

Their mother was making the evening meal in the kitchen, humming to herself. The telephone rang, but went unanswered. This being the end of the summer, he persuaded his mother and father to set up a table outside. They would eat in the garden for a change, all four of them, while the ants worked in their underground chambers, tunnelling and whispering their secrets.

MICHAEL MUNRO

APPLICATION

The kettle switched itself off the boil with a sharp click. The young man filled the teapot with the steaming water and dropped in a teabag to succour the one already there. He sat the full pot on the formica-topped breakfast bar and made a silly face at his five-year-old daughter who was perched on a stool slowly getting through a bowl of milky porridge. Hearing his wife coming down the stairs from the bathroom he began to refill her mug but instead of entering the bright warm kitchen she lingered in the hall. He could hear her pulling on her heavy coat. She came in saying she had no time, she'd be late for her lift, her heels clattering on the tiled floor. She kissed goodbye to daughter and husband then was off in a whirl of newly applied perfume and the swish of her clothes and the front door slamming.

He sat down on his stool and poured himself another mug of tea. He asked the child how she was doing, was the porridge too hot? She told him gravely that it was OK and went on making a show of blowing on each hot spoonful as she had been shown.

He picked up the newspaper that was lying folded open at the Situations Vacant pages. One advert was targeted in a ring of red felt-tip pen. The come-on was in big bold italics: *'This time last year I was made redundant. Now I own a £50,000 house, drive a BMW and holiday in Bali. If you . . . '* He opened out the paper and refolded it to the front page to check the headlines. The date he knew already but there it was plain and remorseless: exactly one year he had been out of work.

Father and daughter chatted brightly as they strolled hand in hand down Allison Street heading for school. She was a talkative child and he would egg her on in her prattle for his own amusement. It was now well into the rush hour: traffic gushed by or fretted at red lights and urgent pedestrians commanded the pavements and crossings. It was bitter cold. He looked down at the girl to reassure himself that she

was warmly enough dressed, but there was no need; he was
well used to getting her ready. Her round reddened face was
the only prey to the cold air and she beamed up at him, quite
content.

At the last corner before the school's street they both
halted in an accustomed way and he squatted down to give
her a kiss. She didn't mind the daily ritual but forbade its
enactment outside the gates: her pals might see and that
would be too embarrassing. He tugged her knitted hat a little
further down her forehead and tucked in a couple of strands
of her long reddish hair. They could hear the kids' voices
laughing and shouting from the playground. They waved
cheerio at the gate and he stood watching until she was inside
and assumed into some little coterie, then he turned away.
He was vaguely aware of one or two mothers doing likewise
and one or two car doors slamming. With both gloveless
hands shoved into the pockets of his cream-coloured raincoat
he made for home. Behind him the bell began to sound above
and through the high excited voices.

He finished writing the letter and signed his name with a
brisk underline, printing it in brackets below, just in case.
Picking up the CV from the coffee table he glanced over its
familiar outlines. It looked good, he thought, organised,
businesslike. His wife had managed to get a couple of dozen
of them run off on her word processor at the office. It was
the contents that struck him as pointless. What use was it to
anyone to know what he had done at school? It was the
grown man, someone with work experience, who was on
offer, not the schoolboy. Not the kid who'd scuffed along,
neither brilliant nor stupid, not the football-daft apprentice
smoker and opportunist drinker who'd put his name to those
long-forgotten exam papers then sauntered out carefree into
the world. Well, maybe not carefree: he could still remember
some of the burdens and terrors of adolescence that he'd
laugh at now, the state he was in now. Then there was his five
years of selling for the one firm. No problem there; those
were good years. Their fruits were holidays abroad, marriage,
the house, the baby. Plain sailing until the company had gone
bust. Now he was no longer classifiable as young and upward-
ly mobile. Not even horizontally mobile: stopped, stuck.

Referees. He always wanted to write 'Tiny Wharton' but
didn't. What did people expect to hear from the names he
always supplied — 'Don't touch this character, he's a definite

no-user'? It was just wee games, this form-filling. He believed it was the interview that would count, if only he could land one.

He ranged the letter and CV together, tapping sides and tails until there was no overlap, then folded them in half and in half again. The envelope was ready, briskly typed by his wife this morning on the old manual machine she used for home typing jobs. As he made ready to lick the stamp he stopped suddenly. Damn! He'd done it again, folding the sheets in half twice. That was clumsy, unprofessional-looking. The way she'd shown him was much better: folding one third then another so that you only had two folds instead of three. Gingerly, he tried to reopen the envelope but it was stuck fast and the flap ripped jaggedly. He'd have to type another one himself in his laborious two-fingered style. He knew he should practise, try to work up some speed and fluency, but he could never face it and always made excuses to his wife and himself for finding other things to do.

His first go had two mistakes and he was painting them over with correcting fluid when it struck him how the white stuff glared reproachfully from the buff envelope. He typed another one, slowly, making sure he got everything right. The CV was no problem, plenty of spares, but the letter would have to be written out again. He didn't hesitate, just took out a clean sheet and smoothed it down.

He kept walking, on past the pillar-box at the corner of their street. That one was definitely unlucky: nothing he had ever offered there had brought good fortune. No, he would carry on to Victoria Road whose business and air of industry made it feel a more hopeful point of departure. As he reached the main thoroughfare he saw a mailvan pull up at the post-box he was heading for and he quickened pace out of his saunter. He watched the grey-uniformed driver jump down and unlock the red door; he broke into a run. Disembowelled, the pillarbox yielded a bulky flow of mail to the driver's hand combing it into his big shapeless bag. The young man handed over his letter with a half-smile although his heart had sunk. One letter in all that flow of paper. And how many were job applications piled randomly, meaninglessly on top of one another. His own would soon be lost in that anonymous crowd. It seemed to him now more than ever like buying a raffle ticket, like backing the coupon every week. What chance had you got?

The red van nosed purposefully out into the mid-morning traffic. Plenty of work for the Post Office anyway. Maybe he could get taken on at Christmas. Christmas! He tried not to think about it but it loomed in the back of his mind like the threat of nuclear war. His digital watch told him, among other things, that he had plenty of time for a walk in Queens Park before the school came out for lunch.

He stumped up the steep tree-shadowed paths towards the summit of Camp Hill, up towards the flagpole. He was concentrating on keeping his footing on the slippery skin of dead brown leaves; his shoes had long since lost their grip. Doing this climb nearly every day had made him feel rather fitter than he used to be. When he'd had the company car his wife would say that he wouldn't walk the length of himself. Fitness was a vogue commodity now, but fit for what? It took a different sort of stamina, the race he was in, round and round in circles till you drop. He was aware of his breath vapouring out in front of him. Maybe the Campsies would have snow on them today.

A big mongrel dog came bouncing towards him, checked in a slither of leaves and claws and came to sniff him enthusiastically. He patted its damp head and laughingly tried to keep its muddy paws off his raincoat. He looked up at the sound of a displeased voice calling the animal to heel. A middle-aged man in a blue car-coat stood there shaking his head resignedly. The young man smiled, said it was OK, he liked dogs. The older man smiled back and paused as if willing to chat. He'd seen him around the park before; he must be early retired or redundant. But the dog was off, crashing through the rhododendrons and its owner cursed half-heartedly, winked and called a farewell before hurrying after his charge.

Within the railed circle at the flagpole the young man encountered only a couple of boys sharing a bench and a cigarette. They should have been at school at this hour. One wore a multicoloured sweater with an expensive brand name. The other had on a light summer jacket, sleeves pushed up to the elbows, and his hands and forearms were red with the cold. They allowed the stranger a dispassionate brief glance before lapsing back into their casually obscene conversation.

The view was a disappointment today. Northwards the edges of the city and the hills he knew to lie beyond were erased by grey walls of mist that merged upward into low cloud. He could just make out the Cathedral's green roof straight ahead and the University's spires off to the west. Victoria Road ran arrow-straight for the city's heart. He could hear, distant, all around, the sound of the city and it seemed to him like the vague roar of a titanic air-conditioner. He watched the cars and buses and lorries bleed in and outward on the main roads.

It was easy now to recall the bustle of business life. Now it was just about lunchtime, when offices and shops would exchange populations with the pubs and restaurants. He could picture his former colleagues about their business lunches: the customers and clients, the mugs and suckers and flymen; the mates, alliances, conspiracies and flirtations, stories and jokes, continental lager and curries and games of squash. He could see their flushed faces, triumphant, sated. It was something to think about: all this unemployment and the town still buzzed with a life that would not be quelled. It came to him how much he wanted it, that activity. It was more than just something you did to make money: it was the only life he knew and he was missing out on it, standing on the sidelines like a face in the crowd at a football game. If it wasn't for the child, he thought, he wouldn't have the will to keep on trying.

He checked his watch again: the kids would soon be coming out.

He waited at their corner, hands deep in pockets, his shoulder to the dirty grey sandstone wall. The bell was ringing and he could hear the children streaming out into the playground. When she spotted him she broke into a trot and he retreated round the corner a little to swoop suddenly with a mock roar, bearing her laughing wildly up into his arms. As he set her down he asked quite formally what kind of morning she'd had. She began to speak, a child's narrative of rushing and halting and her enthusiasm breathed upwards into his smiling face and beyond in the chill air.

GAVIN SPROTT

THE SUMMER HOUSE

Like his father and grandfather before him, Will Gibson was a joiner to trade. He lived at Springbank with his wife and family. The place lay at the roadside, sitting into the sun, just that few feet high enough off the bottom of the Howe to give a clear view across to the Sidlaws rising on the southern side. At the back of the house, also flanking the road, was the rambling assembly of sheds where the work was done, and at the front and far side lay the garden. Behind Springbank was a small stand of mature trees, the beech and plane trees so typical of Angus, the one with its flaky scaling bark, the other with the smooth tarnished silver on which children and lovers readily carve their names.

Although it stood by itself, Springbank was not isolated. Seventy yards down the road on the other side was the smiddy. Although the attached pendicle was known as Howdie's Croft after some old usage, the place was known just as the Smiddy, or more grandly as Canaan Smiddy, after the nearby village.

Why Canaan, nobody was certain. It sounded strange in a land of either ancient Pictish names or simple Scotch ones, or even the occasional place set up by a laird and called for his wife or daughter. It was said the village had first been a settlement of weavers, and being religious bodies who fancied they were following in the steps of the Israelites, it got that name.

Will Gibson was a busy man, so busy he scarce had time to attend to one of his principle interests, the garden that ran down the side of the road from the front of the house. Its arrangement followed a well used pattern. In the height of summer the borders of the beds were solid with the flourish of gilliflowers, sweet william and such like. The smaller shaded corners had lush cushions of violets, *Kirrie dumplins* — what passed locally for variegated primulae of Will Gibson's own breeding, the successors of the delicate springtime *spinkies*. Beyond this phalanx of flowers were solid ranks of leeks, onions, greens and Will Gibson's main horticultural interest, his potatoes. An admirer of the great Paterson, he sought to

emulate him in a minor way, aiming to produce a cross between a native red and the new imported Chiloe Garnet. This
was what made the garden at Springbank curious and caused
people to pause by the roadside, remarking on the little canvas
pokes with which he shrouded the flowers to keep out his
bees and control the pollination himself, in his aim to produce his own *tattie aipples*. The problem that attended this
project was getting the Reds and the Garnets to flower at the
same time.

The difficulty in finding time for this interest was not
owing to the pressure of work, but because he had so many
other interests. He not only had his bees, but his livelihood.
Although that might have been described as his work, that
would not have given a true picture, for there was no distinction between that, his tatties and his bees. He applied
himself to all his interests with the same industrious ab-
sorption. He would eye the wheel of a cart as a musician
might turn a strange fiddle in his hands. He could turn out
the fine wheel of a gig or dog-cart with its long elegant spokes
crowding in a neat pattern onto the slim nave, or just as easily
a cart wheel which was as handsome as it was strong. 'Man,'
folk said, 'hou d'ye nae mak somethin o't?', indicating that he
could do a good business as a coachbuilder. 'Oa, it's juist for
fun' he would reply with his ironical smile. Only at certain
aspects of cabinetmaking did he draw the line. Not only was
it difficult for an outsider to come by certain secrets of that
trade, but the notion of veneers did not appeal to him. He
liked things to be as they seemed, with no distinction between the appearance and the substance.

'There's a message fae the big hous.'
'Oa ay.'
'Fae the leddy. She wants ye til redd up her simmer hous.
Some fancy notion 'at she has.'
'Ay.'
'She wants ye til ging up by and she'll hae a word wi ye.'
'I'm shair.'
'Fan 'll ye ging?'
'Oa, sometime, — fan I get a chance, like.'
Will's wife Mary gave him an arch glance. If people wanted
a job done in reasonable time, as often as not it was her they
came to, with a 'message' for Will. 'Get Mary til hae a word
wi him' was the simple formula. It was not that Will Gibson
was unapproachable — rather the opposite. Gentle in his

manner, once his interest was aroused in something, — 'ou ay,
we'll gie't a thocht' he would say: and he would chew it over
in his mind with a thoroughness that could drive others to
distraction. 'A dour stuck-up kind o' a cratur' some said, mis-
taking his reflectiveness for arrogance.

'I tell't her ye'd ging up the morn.'

'Thanks for lattin 's ken.'

'Weil, dinna stert. Ye ken fat like the laird is. He winna
thole ony delay.'

'I thocht ye said it was his leddy.'

'Ay. And she's waur, a pettit bairn, juist.'

'Weil, dammit, I'll ging up ee nou. I'll nae be nailed doun
like that.' He rose from the table and picking his bonnet off
the lug of the chair as he passed, ambled out of the room.

'Fat's til dae wi ye m'n' she muttered at his back. 'I
canna get ye til dae somethin for weeks, and ye're up and
awa like a bird for nae guid cause ava.'

It was indeed a fine evening. With only two weeks to mid-
summer, the sun was still well above the hills to the west,
even at six o'clock. Will Gibson looked in at the open doors
of the big shed as he passed. A new made cart stood complete
in fresh paint, the shafts raised on the resting pole, the shel-
vins in position, the whole painted a mid green with the spectacle design on the front board in red. The lettering on the
oval plate on the right side of the cart read 'James Rennie,
Meikle Pow' and 'No. 3' in the middle. The lettering, in pale
golden yellow, was as sharp as if it had been embroidered.
The crisp new ironwork gleamed fresh black with a dull gloss,
catching the level rays of the sun. Gibson tested the hardness
of the paint on the sliders with his thumb nail. Although it
would be back to the bare metal within a minute of the cart
being yoked, that did not matter. Will Gibson insisted that
his carts cross the threshold of his workshop 'like a new
prein'. He never put his name on them. 'A'body kens our
cairts' he would say to his laddies and Bob and Sam, the two
journeymen, would nod their agreement.

Walking up the road, he noted with satisfaction that the
bees were still flying. They were doing well off the clover
this year, but that was not the main preoccupation of his
thoughts, as he walked quietly up the road. He had just got
hold of one of the hexagonal hives that they used in the Kil-
maurs district of Ayrshire, complete with supers and brood
chamber. The beauty of the construction and design and its
apparently perfect adaptation to the habits and life of the

black Scotch bee had caught his imagination. To some, bees were angry and dangerous insects, but to Will Gibson they were gentle and industrious creatures that he handled with confidence and affection.

The *big hous* was an old tower house with various additions. He was as familiar with it as the inside of one of his own hives. New sash cords and the like he left to Sam or Bob, but when the lady had a *notion*, he knew that nothing less than his own presence would do.

In fact, she was one of the few people whose advice he would take seriously. He had made various bits of furniture for her, — cabinets, tables, chairs and a writing desk. She had not only admired them, but had put into words a mutual understanding of their quality — the definition of the lines, the bold flow of the curves, and the way the design emphasised the strong clean character of the natural timber. She had noticed the half-hidden streaks of golden green in the wych elm, and the graceful ebb and flow of the grain in the ash. She had opened the small drawers in the writing desk and pushed them back softly, noting the precision with which they shut flush and square, riding home on a cushion of expelled air. Some items she had given away as wedding presents. 'You know, Gibson, you're quite an artist' she had said on one occasion.

'Eigh?' Will Gibson had adjusted his bonnet. She had only smiled, and shaken her pretty head.

The summer house stood on the edge of a beech wood about three hundred yards from the castle. Some old yews formed a little bower around one side and rhododendrons on the other. With a small foundation and base course of stone, the rest was of timber. Gibson approached it and halted twenty yards away, sizing it up. 'Ane orrie Chinese like o' a thing' he mused to himself. 'They'll hae some job gettin new tiles til thon ruif.' It looked silly and out of tune with the old castle and everything else in the policies. Gibson went right up to it, and taking a small pocket-knife, jabbed the timber at various critical points. Rotted! At least that gave him the night to think about it.

Just as he turned to go, he was surprised when she herself emerged from the little building.

'Ay Mem.' His hand went up to readjust his bonnet, his habitual reaction to puzzlement or surprise, He thought she looked slightly flustered.

'Oh Gibson, it's you! I couldn't think what that thumping noise was. I didn't expect you so soon.'

'I'd caa this doun and big anither ein' he replied bluntly. 'Juist yaise the auld founds. Had ye onythïn in mind, Mem?'

'Well, that's what I'll discuss with you. Now is not convenient. Come up tomorrow at eleven.'

Gibson thought he detected an unaccustomed note of sharpness. 'Ay Mem' he said, and walked off at a quicker rate than usual. Thirty paces away he turned on impulse and glanced back. As well as the lady standing in the doorway he saw a man. It was not the laird, and in that instant before the face disappeared, he could see them smiling at each other, and even in his innocence, Gibson knew that they were lovers. He strode away at a sharp pace, burning with indignation and embarrassment. 'The ae time ye dae a thing on the nail' he thought 'and ye come on the likes o' that.'

Except that the word *lovers* was not directly in his mind. At the capers, a bit nibble on the side, houchmagandie, — that was the standard vocabulary. He stopped. Fat's the haste? Going over to a dyke he lit his pipe and leaned over. Oa, she'll nae fash hersel. Fat the servants and ither fowks sees disna count, — like they was dumb baests. Then this mood of irritation gave way to amusement. His cousin had been at the station at Perth when the royal party had arrived. Awaiting them had been a long rake of carriages. He had asked a porter who was going to fill them all? 'That's for the royal bastards' had been the solemn reply, 'they aye ging about wi them.' His humour thus restored, Gibson walked down the road, applying his thoughts to what he would do with the summer house 'fae the founds up'.

The bairns met him on the road back. They were barefoot and hazed with the dirt of the day's play they got between the little jobs he gave them. He clapped them on the back and ruffled their hair as he might a big dog, and noted their bright eyes and healthy colour with pleasure. 'Ye've gotten a richt skud abuin yer ee' he remarked to Chae, his eldest son.

'That was Eckie. He was gaein awa til rive the hin shanks aff o' a puddock and I said he shouldna and I'd fecht him for't.'

'Fat become o' the puddock?'

'Oa, it juist lowpit awa.'

They all laughed, and chatting about other things they reached Springbank.

'Time ye was beddit, bairns' he remarked quietly at the

garden gate. His own four vanished into the house and the others made down towards the smiddy and the village. A simmer hous for simmer's day. Faa bides in simmer houses onywye? Naebody, but they hae their yisses, seemingly. Presently he heard the sharp note of Mary's voice, and for the second time that day he felt a stab of irritation. 'Ach, haud yer damned wheist' he said out loud to himself, and turned to go in.

By the time she arrived, Will Gibson had the thing worked out in his head, including the price. Carts, wheelbarrows, scythe sneds, coffins, you didn't have to work them out, they were standard. But building work you did, and as Gibson well knew, everybody was as interested in the price as the meanest farmer. The only difference was they weren't all as mean.

She arrived slightly late, greeting him with a quick business-like smile.

'Good morning Gibson. Now, what can you do with this summer house?'

'Like I said, caa it doun and big a new ein. Ye could raise the framin o' the main uprichts, but the lave o't 's fell shachlie. And yon ruif, — it's duin, and it's faur ower heavy for the size o' yon place. I had a word wi Tam Wedderburn the builder on the road up, but he says he couldna get the like o' yon fantoush things, — the tiles, like — nae place. Faur d' they come fae onywye?'

'I don't know exactly. This was built by my husband's grandfather about fifty years ago. He had spent much of his life in the far east. Maybe he actually had them sent home.'

'Ay. Weil, that explains it. They fund they didna hae tiles eneuch, sae they hackit doun the size o' fat they had in mind til yon daft wee thing. It's aa out o' balance, Mem.'

'You know, you're quite right, Gibson. And that's just what's happened. What can you do about it?'

'I suppose they'd hae a shot at makin yon tiles speicial ower at Inchcoonans in the Carse, a'though I dout it 'ad be fell costly.'

'Don't worry about that.'

'Eigh?' Gibson's hand went up to the skep of his bonnet, causing it to slide discreetly about the crown of his head.

'No, this is something special for me.'

'Speicial, Mem? A'weil.' He paused for a moment, then bending and scooping some gravel from the ground, he started laying out the little stones in shapes and patterns on the step.

'See, Mem, here's yer founds and uprichts 'at ye've got. Dae awa wi yon ruif, like sneddin the tap fae an egg. Get shot o' aa that daft whigmaleeries atwein yer uprichts, Nou, pit in windaes wi a nice airch, kirkie like, and cairry the astragals through like that, sae's they cross wi a diamond mitre. Nou, the windaes 'll come abuin the auld easin, sae ye dae awa wi't, and big a new ein.'

'What about the roof then?'

'Ah-weil! — reed. I could dae't wi reed theik. It 'ad flow aesy and saft ower the rigs and furs ye'd get wi yon windaes. It 'ad luik richt bonny. Ye could croun it wi some fancy bit tourie for fun. Div ye ken fat I mean, Mem?'

'Gibson, you're a marvel. I'll leave it to you.'

'But fat about the price, Mem?'

'Oh, just charge up the expense. It's the time I'm concerned about. Can you do it as quickly as possible.' This was not a question, but a polite order.

'I'll dae fat I can, Mem.'

'You see, this is important to me. Something personal.'

Gibson nodded and turned to go.

'You saw there was someone else here last night?'

Gibson turned back towards her, his face impassive. 'Na Mem, I didna see naethin.'

'Oh but you did, and I think we understand one another.'

'A'weil — ay.'

'Can I trust your discretion? That is not a thing I can command of you — only ask it as of one person to another.'

'Shairly. But ye'd nivver hae onything til fear fae me.'

'Thank you. I am grateful.'

'Ach, dinna mention it. It's yer ain affair.'

This rejoinder might have seemed blunt and cheeky, but it wasn't, and she knew it. Their eyes met briefly, and as he finally turned to go, she saw in the corner of his mouth the flicker of a kindly smile.

Will Gibson always worked to a definite rhythm. Never idle, he moved at a sedate pace that seemed beyond his thirty five years. Even his occasional wrath had an indrawn quality, reaching its crescendo and dissipation through a long steady tramp. Once asked by Mary if he had got over a bad mood, he replied dourly that she should observe what happened with foul weather — 'it's aye gaed aff afore.' So people could be forgiven the licence of a little exaggeration when they said that 'he's gaed clean daft ower thon simmer hous'. As he remarked, 'there's nae muckle mair in't nor the makin o' a cairt wi a frame and neip creils'. The reason was because he did most of the intricate work himself, even by lamplight after the summer light had failed, running the mouldings and cutting and fitting the difficult mortice and tenon joints where the curving astragals crossed.

However, a little six-sided summer house was not so little when it came to making four windows and their frames, a glazed door, and the framing for the eaves and the roof besides the internal furnishings. He had to send a cart away down to Port Allan to get reeds for the thatch, and get Jim Boag the smith to make the hinges, latches, and window furnishings as he wanted.

Yet within a week most of the work was done, and going up with the cart and his men, Gibson had the roof off and the old building reduced to a rudimentary shell in a day.

While Sam and Bob reared the new structure, Gibson spent much of the time standing back and eyeing it as it took shape. The lady was not long in coming by.

'Good Lord!' she exclaimed. 'How have you done it so quickly?'

'Aa the fancy bits we did in the shop. This is the aesy bit.'

'Like putting together a puzzle. But it's not a puzzle to you, is it?'

'Na Mem, but ye're aye learnin.'

She gave him a sideways glance. 'About what?' She had caught something in his expression, but he did not rise to it, only an almost undetectable lift of an eyebrow. 'What gave you the idea?' she continued.

'I fancied somethin different, juist' he replied, after a pause.

'You speak in riddles. Not that I don't understand them.'

This time he looked at her, not sidelong, but directly, and she felt a mild shock at his intelligent stare. He nodded shortly, and going over to join the others lifted his bevel and rule and started working.

There was other work to do, so Will Gibson worked on the thatch alone. There was no mystery about it, only as he put it, 'aesy til dae course, hard til dae weil'. Working from a ladder, he secured the sheaves of reeds to the battens with their binder twine, and tied lesser bundles in between them, and working upwards beat the ends in to make an even surface

with an old plumber's mell. He had made a little hexagonal
cap of larch for the top, and had just secured it down by
a redwood finial that he had turned, when he heard her
call from below. Glancing down over his shoulder, he eyed
her in her long white summer dress, with her parasol cocked
playfully over her shoulder. There was something of the child
in her, and catching her mood he smiled, and then despite
himself, his features broke into a grin. Coming down the
ladder he lifted it off, and laying it aside strode a good twenty
paces back until he had a good view of the building. She
came and stood beside him, and raising her fingertips placed
them together in an unconscious and lighthearted parody of
thanksgiving.

'Who would have thought it could be so beautiful?' she
said. 'You should make things like that all the time.'

He said nothing, but going back to the little building held
open the door for her. There was still a scent of new sawn timber and smell of fresh paint. But she stopped just inside the door
and gave a cry of surprise. In the middle was a small six-sided
table left in the natural pine and lightly oiled, and on it lay a
bunch of wild flowers, — columbine, woodbine, bluebells,
wood hyacinths. 'That's for hansel, Mem' he said. His voice
sounded solemn, but when she looked, she saw in his face a
darting wildfire of gaiety. 'Weil, that's it' he added in his
matter-of-fact voice, and going out he shouldered his ladder.

'Oh, — thank you' she said earnestly, staring after him.

The saga of the summer house was soon forgotten with
the approach of harvest. While the countryside lay quiet in
the late August sun, the workshop at Springbank echoed to
the rasp of the saw and the clatter of hammer and mallet
from first light well into the evenings — bosses for stackyards,
reels, flights and poles for reapers and the new binders, repairs for carts and harvest frames, sneds for scythes and a
hundred other small things. Yet there was time enough for
Will Gibson to contemplate his failure to cross the Garnets
with the Red tatties, and to take satisfaction in the progress
of his Stewarton hives and make arrangements to take them
up to Lumlie Den for the heather.

The days shortened into September, still hot enough at
noon, but with a nip in the air by nightfall. The harvesters
were out, first in the barley, then the few parks of wheat on
the carse ground, then the acres of corn, burnished to a deep
burnt gold. By that time they were already leading the first

of the barley, the farm tracks and country roads sounding
with the jingle of draught chains, the stertorous clump of the
horses, and the rumble and creak of carts half hidden under
their ample loads of sheaves. Meanwhile the machines worked
in the fields, their reels nodding round like prayer wheels,
sweeping the crop into the chattering knives. Round all this
swarmed the population, a weary cheerful army, binding,
stooking, forking, stacking from first light until last.

Will Gibson and his family went down to give Jim Boag a
hand at the Smiddy croft. Three acres of corn was nothing
among the surrounding big farms, but it had to be taken down
with the scythe. The two men worked together in easy rhythm,
the rusty blades of their scythes soon burnished bright as
they flashed under the straws, the women and older children
following, binding and stooking and the younger ones and
the dogs racing back and fore after rabbits, game and vermin
that bolted from the diminishing crop. After them all a contented little flock of hens fanned out over the fresh stubble,
feasting on the shaken grain. Jim Boag cursed when at inter-
vals he was called away to sort some vital bit of machinery,
and Will Gibson worked on with the scythe by himself.

Early on the second day they were threatened with rain,
rising in the morning to find half the stooks scattered. The
small storm had died away to stillness in the early morning,
making way for heavy dew. Carrying the sheaves under their
arms to set them up again, they were soaked in minutes. But
as the sun climbed up, the flanks of their breeks and shirts
dried out and their backs ran with sweat. The men stopped
now and again for a draught of mealy water. At ten they all
stopped and gathered for a break.

'Weil, if we're nae hindered we'll hae't feinished gin aftir-
nuin' said Jim Boag.

'Ay. An that'll be anither hairst' added Gibson.

'Awa m'n, ye hivna led it yit.'

'I mind eince at the Dron leadin shaefs on Christmas day.'

'Nae muckle o' a crap that, shairly.'

'Na, ye'd be surprised.'

And so they chatted. The conversation drifted along. Will
Gibson eyed the little circle, the children still capering despite
their exertions, Mary munching her scone. Oa, it's a necessity,
he mused, breid til wer mouths. Fat can ye say?

'Fat's come ower ye, m'n! Ye'll nae get things duin at
that rate.'

Gibson started out of his reverie, In fact, he was the first back to work, swaying to his scythe as the crop reishled and crackled before him, the swathes toppling beside him in a continuously breaking wave. The pain had gone out of his back and arms. It was somewhere inside him, an ache pulling at his heart that he could not place.

That evening there was a listlessness about the place. The bairns had been squabbling, and in the end Gibson ordered them all off to bed.

'It's nae their time yit. They'll nae get sleepit' said Mary.

'God wumman, fat wye d'ye counter 's. D'ye nae want some peace yersel? Hae ye naethin til dae else nor heid yon racket?'

'Plaese yersel.'

'Ye can dae likewyse. I'm gaein til tak a turn out.'

She said nothing, watching him go with a dumb stare.

He tramped up the road onto the little ridge behind Springbank, and at an accustomed spot stopped to kindle his pipe. The land lay quiet in the gloaming, the bulk of the Sidlaws blackening by the minute, the coppery yellow pinpricks of lamps rising in the dark shapes that were cottar-houses and farm-touns, with little spangled concentrations where the villages lay. It seemed the whole world basked in a contented weariness except perhaps, himself. His eye worked over the ground, the little hollows, the lie of the burns, the run of the roads and tracks, the familiar names coming to mind. Then he stopped and narrowing his eyes, concentrated his vision on a spot about a mile distant. Inconspicuous during the day, it now stood as a little lighthouse in its clearing, the trees rising around it like the crags of a shore. It seemed strange. He considered for a moment, them slowly he walked towards it, not along the road and up the drive but across the stubbly parks, between the stooks, along the edges of the woods and over dykes. Bats tumbled in the air and the occasional owl made its silent vigorous flight across his path. At one point he noticed poachers in the distance. They were netting partridges, but melted away at his approach, taking him for a keeper.

Coming up to the summer house, he saw that she was there alone, sitting reading by the light of a single oil lamp. It was not like the ones that most people had, but burnt with an incandescent mantle, giving a bright, almost harsh, lemon light. He gave a gentle tap at the door. She looked up with a start.

'Who is it? Come in.'

'Ay Mem. I was out for a dander, juist, and seen yon licht.
I thocht I'd tak a luik at the place.'

'Well Gibson, you made it, so who would deny you that?
Come in and sit down.' She indicated the window seat opposite herself. 'Your summer house has been lovely' she continued. 'I suppose you saw the light. Unusual to sit in a
summer house with a light.'

'I seen it by chance. It seemed strange, ay. Simmer's ower
nou.'

'Too true, Gibson. Summer's over now. I haven't read a
word of this book. I came here to think — before I lock the
door.'

'There's nae a sneck on the door, Mem.' Gibson shook his
head, surprised that she had never noticed. 'It didna seem —
that kind o' a place — for snecks and bolts and that, — ken
fat I mean?'

'Yes. That kind of a place.'

'A'weil, I suppose that juist the wye o't.'

'Is it?' The habitual self control of her breeding faltered,
her voice becoming husky. 'What is that, Gibson, your country-
man's wisdom?'

He shook his head earnestly. 'Na Mem. That's juist — the
wye o't' he repeated helplessly. 'Things are the wye they are.'

'That was a liberty. Yes, you are right. The way things
are, neither for us nor against us. But do we just let life happen
to us?'

'Hou should I ken, Mem?'

'I don't know. You must speak for yourself.'

'It was yersel 'at pit the question, Mem.'

'Even so, why dodge it?'

Gibson shrugged his shoulders. 'I'm juist the jyner. I mak
things.'

'What do you make for yourself?'

'Nae muckle.'

'Kind man — but as sharp as a fox, you catch the scent of
things. Like a little cathedral this place, isn't it? — but light,
airy and cool. Voices made perfect in this little shape, features
made perfect in the evening light of your window. Heavens,
Gibson, why am I telling you this!'

'Because the simmer's ower, Mem.'

She drew in a sharp breath and tried to speak, but she
couldn't. Threatened by tears, she shook her head in a single
sharp movement to the side as if to free herself.

Gibson rose and grasping the lamp by the base, unscrewed

the cap on the filling hole. The flame flared, blackening the mantle as he moved it, tipping it over, the oil spilling out of the side onto the floor and the seat he had just left.

'Good Lord, what are you doing man! Have you gone mad?'

Gibson motioned her to the door with a curt nod of his head, and she scampered past him in a panic. He replaced the half-emptied lamp on the table and reaching into his pocket drew out a box of matches. He went over to the door, his face impassive, and striking a match flicked it into the pool of liquid. For a moment the little flame struggled for life, drowning in the oil, then it caught, running, leaping, galloping up the timber work with a roar. Casually he walked away from the building, turning on the spot where the two of them had regarded his handiwork on that June afternoon. She paced up to him in a fury. 'My summer house, how ... how dare you!'

He shook his head, ironical, unperturbed. 'Yer simmer hous? I nivver sent nae account.'

'But ... that's preposterous!' She gaped at him with incredulity, her eyes wide, her cheeks puffed up as she blew out a long slow breath. She turned and faced the blaze, speechless, as the flames raged inside. It was spectacular, and as she watched, fascinated, gradually her features relaxed to a curious calm. As the glass shattered, the flames leapt outside and gripping the thatch at the eaves, exploded into a crackling white column, sending a fierce jet of ragged sparks up into the blackness.

She glanced around, looking to see if some of the servants would come running from the castle or the estate cottages, but none appeared. The blaze could be seen from afar, but from all those nearby it was hidden. In minutes it was over, settling back to a modest bonfire of fallen timber where the table had been, the odd blue flame limping over the glowing shrunken surface of the surviving uprights.

Although shaken, her voice was natural and her own. 'The next summerhouse you must build for yourself.'

'Me — faur about?'

'In yourself.'

He stood silent, frowning at the ground. The final understanding came by degrees. It was still new to him. 'Ay' he said at last, 'true.'

At the same instant they both turned to go their ways.

DILYS ROSE

PANDORA

I'm sick of this second-hand life,
waiting for you to come rollicking home
drunk on glory and fit for nothing.
It's all very well, this mansion,
the patio, the expansive view
of blue sea. My suntan
is even. The waiter brings drinks
on cue. I don't deny my luck —

it's just — for weeks I've watched
figs darken and swell. I've wished
at the golden well and waved to boats
in the bay. Not any more. Bored,
I've taken to sleeping most of the day
and taught myself to dream at will,
though even that has palled. All
I dream about is this same place,

its gorgeous monotony, its glut
of luxury. Looked at too long, gilt
dulls. And food has no taste, heat
no warmth, rest no respite. Daily,
I unlock doors, rummage in caskets,
trunks, all except one, itching
to lift the forbidden lid. Perhaps
if I did, you'd stay at home more often.

SISTER SIRENS

Another boat veers for the perch
where we're tethered.
We preen our feathers,
croon seductive duets —
the sailor is deaf to all else.
He ignores omens,
throws sense to the wind
sets course for the harbour
of our twin smiles.
The moon conspires with us
upgrades our allure.
How gorgeously we glimmer.
Our glamour takes his breath away.
If only I'd squawked a warning —
beauty is only a trick of the light,
beneath our flightless wings
we've talons to tear out your heart —
if only I screeched, 'Block up your ears,
cover your eyes, if need be, bind yourself
to the mast.' More monster than myth —
we'll pick you clean.
Later we'll toss on this rocky bed,
unable to sleep.
We'll gossip and bitch,
squabble over whose good looks
charmed him ashore. But to ourselves
curse the gods who blessed us with
the songbird's voice, the hawk's claw.

LAURNA ROBERTSON

INHERITED RINGS ON INHERITED FINGERS

Grandfather's great-grandfather,
Press-ganged behind the headland,
His oarless boat found drifting,
Fought at Trafalgar. His daughter,
Wearing black for her eldest son,

Haunted the pierhead shipping office
Till his ship limped, three months late
Into Valparaiso, sails torn to shrouds
By tons of ice, a winter prison
Rounding Tierra del Fuego.

Governess in Petersburg, great-grandmother,
Whose gloved hand could not span an octave,
Rocked on the railway from Russia
A trunk of music in Gothic type
That none since she has mastered.

My blue-eyed grandfather, dead at thirty,
Left his boy to wait by the kitchen door;
Striped canvas curtains moving slightly,
Smells of cooling gingerbread taunt an old man
Still holding his father's giant bicycle.

I rummage the attic for clues
To the characters beyond cameos.
Raising box-lids I find skeins of coiled hair
Saved from my great aunts' hairbrushes
To swell their Edwardian top-knots.

And curling, unframed photographs;
Groups caught off guard by a sudden shutter.
Whispers and silences. Inherited rings
On inherited fingers. A nerve bead
Which beats, here in my temple.

SIX POEMS

NO RIGHT TO REMAIN SILENT

The worse for too much
drink and life
he bent down,
kneeling in rain,
to speak to the postbox.

All down the street
shops were closing,
shutting him out.

He said
what he had to say, waited
and waited; there was no reply.

Above and beyond
where our actions
have no equal and opposite reaction,
a thousand stars lit up the night; you could
easily read the mind of a postbox by it.

ONE SUNDAY AFTERNOON AT CATTERLINE

On a domestic level
it had taken years of spring cleaning
to root it out, to scrape off the varnish,
to catch sight of anything remotely like
that fresh, crisp, dazzling quartz
and mica that broke into branch into breeze.

One Sunday afternoon at Catterline I
understood the conversation
of Christian rocks
and religious sea;
witnessing this conversion
of energies, I realised
how immense the task
of putting nothing back
into its rightful place
would always be.

GUESTS AT THE WEDDING RECEPTION

I saw a man who was a ghost,
white, melting
through tables and chairs and time
in a long room
with music laid from one end to the other
and people, dancing.

I had been a half-truth for so long,
waiting to be found out
(never dreaming
  I would never be found out)
that the moment, when it came, came to pass,
looked back, turned once, and could not be grasped.

There is little profit in logic, and some loss.
Not even a word to my father for twenty odd years.
When they come to close the books
they will not balance.
When the music ends and the room
has cleared, that other, stiller, dance, carries us on.

VICTORIOUS STORM

You were the first to wake;
I had a sense of you, there, tensed
by the window, against a merest tear
in the curtain of darkness.

Then I heard it, batter,
battering, a gate, taken
by the storm and hurled against
some wall, again, again, again.

Held in that bated breath buckle of night,
wondering what and where and if the whole street
     was now
half awake, half asleep, suddenly knowing nothing,
     completely, like this.

When morning came, defeated, perfectly calm,
all gates were shut, night lay behind sealed lips;
     at breakfast
eyes focussed on a few of the hundred usual things.

CAIRN AT SKAIL, STRATHNAVER

A few sheep
can easily fill
the endless time
of this age in its place.

Nothing goes to waste;
the rock breeds
tough tussock,
no frills.

An iron age is all but grown over,
the humpbacked earth a charred midden
where broken glass tells only
of the tinker's curse settling on us.

A soul can easily burn
away to nothing.
Surely with muck as thin as this it took little
to rive up the roots of three hundred men.

KEENING

Keening in its shine the tractor
is a toy, brand new; hand
cupfulled idling daylight
plays a daze across rib-raised furrows.

Tender and sudden the plough tin-opens
hard frostbitten eggshelled fields,
rips into last year,
the past that was buried opens up.

Smoke black arrivals of
cow-heavy cloud hang, slow, overladen
with their own bewildered being,
big bullies, unwilling to move on.

We wait around for evening
to pick up the dice, to find
the missing pieces of some puzzle; used blades
still have the stinging singing edges they have stilled.

DOROTHY K. HAYNES

THE WOBBLY CASTLE

The castle stood by the esplanade, its towers like ice cream cones, its walls a lurid brick colour. It was made of rubber, and pumped up every morning to the proper pressure. At night, with the moon behind it, it really did look like a castle, its silhouette solid against the silver of the sea. In the daytime it was tawdry, a giant balloon with a painted doorway and an inner courtyard corrugated like an enormous li-lo; and on this rust coloured floor the children jumped and screamed and rolled about in ecstasy, while the whole structure shuddered and quivered grotesquely.

'Come and jump on the wobbly castle. Only 20p. Jumping time 5 minutes minimum.' So said the big sandwich board on the pavement, and so said the big man in the linen hat, bawling against the din of the giant Whizzer and the chair-o-planes. Grey shingle stretched beyond the funfare, and the waiting children sat around, barefooted, ready to rush in when the five minutes was up.

'How about this, then?' said aunt Louisa. 'Would you like to jump on that?'

Barbara nodded, and her aunt looked relieved. So far, Barbara had not behaved as a child on holiday should. She would not join in, she dragged back from violent roundabouts, she said 'No, thank you' to everything. Louisa, who felt responsible for giving her niece a good time, was on the verge of irritation. Surely there was *something* the child would enjoy.

Even now, having agreed to five minutes in the castle, the child hung back. She worried about taking her shoes off, she was afraid of the rough, shouting boys who seemed to take up all the room; but her aunt promised to look after her sandals, and lifted her firmly on to the shaking floor.

The floor was hot, and smelt of new tyres. Barbara put out a foot carefully, lurched and fell, and bounced up again. It didn't hurt a bit. This time she jumped, and was surprised how easy it was. After a few more jumps, higher each time, she tried to stride forward, over the undulating floor, and falling and giggling like the others, she staggered, rolled, and lay on her back as the floor billowed and the walls wiggled like jelly.

'Can I go on again, auntie?' she said when the five minutes were up. 'Can I? I want to jump right up to the top.'

'Well, yes, I suppose so. But don't make yourself sick.' At least, thought Louisa, I've found something she likes.

The second time round, she had more confidence. She fixed her eyes on one of the towers, the only one with a window, and tried to reach the narrow black cleft. It was harder than she thought. It was only in the last minute that she sprang right up and, for a long second, looked into the slit of the window.

She was so amazed that when her feet touched the tilting floor she ran stumbling to get off, just as the man was shouting, 'C'mon, kids, your time's up. 20p. for another turn!' She gripped his arm, feeling the ground too flat and too steady. 'Please sir, please — how did the lady get in?'

He looked down at her as he collected the money and shepherded the new lot of jumpers on. 'What lady, love?' he asked. 'And where?'

'In the tower. Looking out of the window.'

He looked at the castle, already dipping and twisting as the children shrieked. 'There's no lady there, pet,' he said. 'It's just a painted window.'

'But it's not! I saw it! I jumped right up, and — '

Come on, Barbara!' her aunt called. 'Come and get your shoes on.'

'Auntie, I saw it! There's a lady in one of the towers. I jumped up and saw her. It's in the window there . . . '

'Just imagination,' laughed the man. 'If I thought there was a lady there I'd be up beside her. You bet your life!' Aunt Louisa ignored him. 'Come on now, Barbara. We'll come back again another day.'

'Auntie, the lady looked as if she wanted to get out. She said "Quick, quick", and she sort of . . . beckoned to me.'

'Now you're making up stories.'

'I'm *not*!'

Aunt Louisa decided that the conversation should end there, and Barbara, being an obedient child, walked along till her aunt let go of her hand and began to fumble for pennies in her purse. 'Would you like some ice cream, dear?'

'Yes, please.' But she loitered as she sucked at her cornet and looked back over her shoulder to where the castle wobbled and gyrated endlessly; and when she went to bed that night she shut her eyes tightly and went over what had happened.

It was no good telling her aunt about it. Kind as she was, she obviously didn't believe it. Nor did the man, but of course *he* could be the one who was keeping her prisoner. He had seemed a nice kind man, but maybe he was only pleasant to children, to get them to spend their money.

As she grew drowsier, everything became clearer and clearer in her mind. She had seen right in, through the iron bars, into a stone flagged room, quite round, with a high carved chair at the window. On the chair sat a sad lady, dressed in black, with a sort of green headdress. One hand, a very narrow hand, crooked a pleading finger through the bars, and the other had what looked like an iron bracelet round the wrist; but when she moved it, painfully, Barbara saw that it was fixed to a thick iron chain, which was fastened to a ring on the opposite wall.

It had only been a glimpse, but she could see the picture in her mind as clearly as if it was painted on a page. It worried her. It was the sort of thing you expected in castles: she had seen plenty of pictures like that in story books, but she *knew* that the castle was only a gigantic balloon.

Next day she emptied her purse and counted her pocket money. She had plenty to pay for quite a few goes on the castle. Aunt Louisa told her to save her money; she'd want to buy things to take home, a present for her mother ... but Barbara was quite firm about it. 'I'm only using *part* of my money, auntie. I just want a good long shot ... '

She did not waste time in aimless jumping or flopping about. She went straight to the tower with the window, and leaped as high as she could. Yes, she was right. The glassless window was barred with an iron grille, but this time there was no face at the window.

She leaped up again, and this time she managed to grab hold of the stone coping. In the few seconds she managed to hold on, she saw that the lady was slumped in a corner, her face in her hands; then she slid down, her hands and knees grazed and nipping.

'For Heaven's sake, Barbara, what have you done with yourself?' said aunt Louisa.

Half crying, half brave, Barbara looked down at the sore areas where the blood was beginning to trickle. 'I got it sliding down the tower,' she said, wincing as her aunt dabbed her with a hankie.

'The tower? But it's as smooth as a balloon!'

'No it isn't! It's rough, and there's a room inside, and the lady's sitting in a corner crying — '

'Right, that settles it,' said her aunt brusquely. 'That's the last time you go on there. And I'm going to see the man about what's wrong with his castle. There must be something dangerous about it for you to get scratched like that.'

But there was nothing wrong with it. The man, impatient, offended, told her to take off her shoes and see for herself; so there was aunt Louisa, trying to be dignified as she lurched along the heaving floor and ran her fingers down every tower in turn.

'I'm sorry,' she said, 'but she *did* hurt herself on something. Don't worry, I'll get the truth out of her yet.'

What Barbara told her, after a lot of firm talking and shaking, *was* the truth, she insisted, but understandably, her aunt didn't believe her. There was an atmosphere for the rest of the holiday, her aunt keeping her busy every minute, and Barbara, too polite to sulk and protest, co-operative but cold. When her mother came to take her home, aunt Louisa had a long talk with her, and after that everyone was bright and cheerful, with thank-yous and goodbyes ringing in their ears after the train had gone.

The castle haunted Barbara. She drew castellated walls and pointed towers in her drawing book, and she searched in her books for any pictures of prisoners in dungeons. At first, her mother did not object. Let her get the thing out of her system, she thought, and she'll forget all about it when she goes back to school. But Barbara did not forget, and so all talk about turret rooms and towers was forbidden. 'Now mind, don't let me hear one more word about it. You should have something better to do than go on about it all day.'

But they could not stop her thinking about it. At night, when the curtains were drawn against the still bright evening, she went over it again and again. She saw the castle against a background of blue sky, she smelt the hot rubbery smell, and she *knew* that the lady pined inside, tethered and maybe tortured. It worried her, got mixed up with her prayers and her mother's bedtime stories, and dominated her dreams. At last her mother, hearing her talk in her sleep, decided to take her back to the seaside, back to aunt Louisa's, so that she could get to the bottom of it once and for all.

It was wet when they arrived, and the fairground was half

empty. 'Wait till you've had your dinner,' said aunt Louisa soothingly. 'Wait till it clears up,' said her mother, with less patience. 'You don't want to go traipsing about in all that rain.'

The rain didn't bother Barbara. As soon as it showed signs of stopping, she coaxed and badgered her mother to come out with her. She did not know that she was under observation. All she knew was that rules seemed to be relaxed, and that she was going to be allowed on the bouncing castle again.

The castle was deserted. Rain filled the creases of the courtyard, and dropped from the blue-capped towers. The man in charge was smoking in a little hut, and he shook his head when Barbara proferred her 20p.

'Sorry, love, No jumping today. Too wet.'

'Oh, but I — '

'It's just an experiment,' her mother said. 'You see, she — she got it into her head there was someone held prisoner here, and I wanted to show her, just to make sure . . . '

The man looked at Barbara, and recognised her, none too pleased at the knowledge. 'Oh aye! The girl that cut herself and said she'd scraped it on the wall.' For a moment, his eyes looked almost vicious, and then he turned to Barbara's mother.

'Well, you see, the trouble is, if I let her on, all the kids'll want on too.'

'Well, they'll pay, won't they?' This was aunt Louisa. 'You're surely not turning away custom?'

'They'll get soaked.' said the man, throwing away his cigarette. 'I'll have their mothers after me. Still, if you say it's all right . . . ' He took the 20p. and lifted Barbara on to the castle. 'Now let's see what you can do.'

The flabby castle didn't wobble so much when there was only one child to rock it. Barbara bounced up and down, self-consciously at first, but later with more confidence. There was no sea sparkling now, nothing but a wet mist seeping down from the sky. Drops of water splashed and trickled as she jumped, and her stockings soaked as she landed on her knees. 'No, it's all right, Missis,' said the man, when her five minutes was up. 'Let her have a bit longer. Looks like she's going to be the only one today.'

She was bouncing higher now, right up to the tower, her hands stretched out towards the bars, and her fingers squeaking on the wet rubber. There was nothing there. The window was a narrow rectangle of black paint, the bars a mere grey tracery.

Puzzled, desperate, she lurched off in her wet stockings and ran to her mother. 'Oh mummy, she's gone! Even the dungeon's gone. But I did see her, I did, I did!' She turned to the man in the linen hat, pleading with him to believe her. 'Where is she? *What have you done with her?*'

The man's eyes twinkled as he got into the spirit of the thing, 'Oh, I set her free. She's working for me, now.'

'Where?'

'In the amusement arcade.' He winked at the adults, preening himself, the man who understood children. 'She's got to behave herself, though. She's got to do what I tell her, or else I'll chain her up again.'

'Oh.' Barbara's eyes went from her mother to her aunt. 'Could we . . . ?'

'Oh come on, we might as well.' Aunt Louisa sighed as rain came on again. 'So long as she doesn't expect us to spend a fortune on her. *I* know these places.'

Barbara dragged her mother along. 'I know the way. It's in here . . . '

'My God!' said her mother. 'Don't tell me *this* is where she spent her time!'

'Oh no!' Aunt Louisa was shocked. 'I wouldn't allow it. Wait till you get inside. It's a lot worse.'

It sounded like bedlam, a battlefield, an illuminated section of hell. Lights flashed, sirens shrieked, there was a taped cacophony of hysterical laughter. Long rows of gaming machines spun and clanked, and occasionally regurgitated a clatter of brown pennies. Flickering screens showed alien planes, bomb bursts, cars going 'splat!' as they crashed off roads. Barbara retreated a little, and then crept in, deafened, mesmerised by the dizzying telegames and the incessant noise.

'Oh, look, mummy! Auntie, look!'

In one corner was an open log cabin with a row of rifles lined up outside. When different targets were hit, dreadful things creaked into motion; a falling window caught an old man by the neck, a corpse came to life and spat derisively, a skeleton reared from a coffin, a door sprang open and ejected a cowboy with a squirting water pistol. Barbara watched in giggling fascination, and even aunt Louisa seemed to enjoy it. 'You know, I used to be quite a good shot,' she began.

'Oh auntie, try it, please try it!' Barbara was now like an ordinary little girl, and her mother began to rummage in her handbag for money. 'No, I haven't got any change.'

'There's a machine over there,' said aunt Louisa, 'Take this pound, pet, and get ten tenpences.'

Barbara skipped away and joined the queue. When her turn came, she clutched the pound and stared, white-faced. There, in a little kiosk no bigger that the room in the tower, sat a woman in black, with a green scarf over her head. She was seated on a high carved chair, and she seemed to have shut her mind to the screaming, bleeping racket around her. As Barbara stared, she put out a languid hand and beckoned desperately. 'Quick, quick!' she said, as the queue behind pushed impatiently. Dazed, Barbara put up her hand with the pound note. The woman pressed a lever automatically, and a rattle of coins racketted down the chute. 'Well, go on, then!' said a boy behind her. Someone scooped up the money and gave it to her, and she stood tranced with her fistful of coins. The woman had had a thick black chain round one wrist . . .

She was still standing there when her mother and aunt Louisa came to look for her.

ANNE ROSS MUIR

JUST A DUMB BLONDE

'There. How do you like it?' Sarah turned her head to the side and surveyed herself critically in the mirror. Behind her, the hairdresser, a young, auburn-haired woman, smiled encouragingly, egging her on to accept what she saw. It was very nice; a soft blonde sheen on her straight hair. Glamorous. 'It'll take a bit of getting used to,' she said doubtfully. The life went out of the hairdresser's smile, so she added hurriedly, 'But you've done a wonderful job. It looks so natural.'

She left a largish tip to compensate for her lack of appreciation, then paid the bill and went to collect her coat from the rack by the entrance. She put it on, buttoning it up automatically, pulling the belt taut with a sharp movement, carefully avoiding the mirror directly in front of her. At the last moment, she glanced up abruptly, catching herself unawares, to see herself as others saw her, as she really was. It worked for a fleeting moment. She saw a woman in her late twenties, pretty, with glorious, golden, shoulder-length hair. She looked unhappy. Sarah glanced round, but the coat rack had been placed in an alcove, and no one could observe her. She turned back to the mirror and tried several adjustments to her expression, to see if she could at least present a happier face to the world. It was a waste of time. No matter how she pulled and twisted her features, her eyes remained intractable. Abruptly, she turned and made for the exit.

Outside, her sudden rush of purposefulness abandoned her. The wind sent a fruit juice carton and some other rubbish scuttling along the pavement and hustled them into the lee of a newsagent's stand, where they eddied on the tideline of the wind. She noticed a torn piece of paper straining at the wire mesh that pinned it to the stand. The headlines proclaimed the war of words building up to the big match that night. Debbie's party. She would need some new tights. On the far side of the street, the rosy-tinted windows of Renner's department store glowed suggestively. She darted across the street and into the shop.

She left by a different door and emerged onto one of the

busy main streets. Pausing by the kerbside, she looked up at the office building opposite. That was where her husband, Martin, worked. The lights were on against the grey weather. She knew his window on the first floor. She could even see his dark head, his white shirt, and then a splash of red as Marge, his secretary, passed by the window. She reappeared behind Martin, placing her hand on his shoulder. Her head bent forward, level with his. Sarah looked away, screwing up her eyes against the grit churned up by the wind.

A few years ago, when they were first married, she used to drop in on Martin's office quite often. Then one day, when she had gone unannounced after a hairdresser's appointment, to see if he was free for lunch, she had stopped off at the toilet on the first floor to repair her make-up. A couple of young women whom she had never seen before, stood by the washbasins, whispering. They started nervously when she entered, but evidently assuming that she was just a casual visitor, they had continued their muttered conversation. Sarah could not help listening, tapping in hungrily to the emotional throbbing of someone else's life. One of the women, with her back to Sarah, was clearly very upset. 'I love him,' she wept. 'Ssh.' The other woman cast a worried glance at Sarah, who was carefully applying foundation cream. Now a grating edge of hatred entered the first woman's voice. 'She's a bitch, just a bitch.' And she broke into sobs. Sarah shifted nervously, now that she could no longer pretend not to hear. Hurriedly, she applied face powder, her gaze skating across the mirror to the image of the pair standing next to her. The second woman hissed impatiently, 'He couldn't give a damn about you ... ' 'He does,' the other's voice rose in protest. 'He said he liked me a lot. He hates his wife. She's neurotic.' Sarah snapped her blusher compact shut.

'He's screwed every typist in this building.'

'But he ... '

'We'd better get back to work or someone'll complain to the agency,' said the second woman with finality. She piloted her companion out of the room, giving Sarah a stretched smile as she passed.

Sarah swept her make-up into her bag. Then she walked out of the room, back along to the lift, pressed to go down and left the building. She never set foot inside the office block again. Nor did she go to any of the business functions, or company parties, if she could help it. Martin accepted her change of behaviour with indifference. She even thought he preferred things that way.

Another gust of wind sent rubbish cluttering around her feet. She checked that she had everything with her . . . bag, gloves, packages and umbrella. She watched a bus loom alongside her, mesmerised by its overwhelming approach, thinking how easy it would be to be sucked into the onrush of wheels. The bus passed and she hurried across the street.

It was five o'clock when she got home. She showered, carefully protecting her hair. Then she sat at the dressing table between the two draped windows and combed out the languorous golden strands. She tilted the side mirrors to see how she looked from all angles. Then she applied her make-up and put on a black dress and the black cobwebby tights she had bought that afternoon. She switched on the bedside lamp, and surveyed herself in the full length mirror. The light clung to her side, highlighting the sheen of her hair and the patina of her silk hosiery that asked to be touched.

She heard the front door burst open and the thudding as Martin raced up the stairs two or three at a time. He had promised to come home early for the party. He swung the bedroom door wide as he entered, tossing his briefcase on the chair, his jacket and tie onto the bed. He seemed to hardly notice her. Within seconds, his muscular body, naked except for a pair of socks, was disappearing into the bathroom and she heard the shower running ferociously. A few minutes later, he emerged, roughly pulling a towel to and fro across his back to dry himself. 'You forgot to get more shampoo,' he said. 'Sorry.' She sat on the dressing table stool, her back to the mirror, watching him. He tossed the towel aside and she leaned forward to pick it up. He pulled on clean underwear and hauled a carefully ironed shirt off the hanger. 'You've got time,' she said mildly. He twisted round from the mirror where he stood buttoning his shirt. 'Hmm?' 'Debbie said about seven but the match doesn't start till 7.30, so we can be a bit late. She's rented one of those video screens.' He regarded her neutrally for a moment, then turned back briskly to the mirror and straightened the collar of his shirt. He reached for a pair of slacks. 'I won't be going,' he said. He watched her in the mirror, but she leant forward so that her hair caught the light, leaving her face in shadow. 'What have you done to your hair?' he asked, disapproval in his voice. 'Highlights,' came the muffled reply. He selected a jacket from the wardrobe. 'It was a last minute thing. Parton invited me to join him and a couple of the directors to watch the match. No wives.' He paused, but still there was no response. Shrugging his shoulders, he reached for the jacket he had discarded and began patting the pockets, until he located his keys. He made for the door, but hesitated as he came level with his wife. She still clasped the wet towel in her lap. Her legs were splayed out from the knees like a schoolgirl's and she sat motionless with head bent. He leaned forward and kissed her quickly on the forehead, stepping back before she could raise her head and lift her arms to put them round his neck. She trailed after him as he went thundering down the stairs, reaching the front door after he had already closed it. From the sitting room window, she could just see his tail lights at the corner before he speeded off into the dusk. The revving engine became fainter and fainter, till finally it was gone. She sat down on the edge of the sofa. She looked round at the milky stillness of the cream walls and carpets. Silence settled on the room like dust. Quickly, she got up, swept her coat from the stand in the hall and left.

It took almost half an hour on the motorway to reach Debbie's house in a quiet, tree-lined street. Several cars were pulled up into the drive, but there was a parking place on the street right in front. She sat in the car for several minutes, watching people with drinks milling around in Debbie's sitting room. Then she started up the car and piloted it out of the line of parked vehicles and drove as quietly as possible to the end of the street. When she glanced in the rear-view mirror, she saw Debbie, standing at the door with a drink in her hand, one leg still trailing over the threshold, watching her. Sarah put her foot down and roared off.

As she swung into the street where she lived, she was astonished to see Martin's car, pulled up onto the verge in front of the house. The front door was standing ajar. She hurried up the two or three steps, swinging her legs round from the knee in an awkward movement because her tight skirt restricted her stride. There were no lights on, and she stopped, uncertain, in the hall. 'Martin?' she called. The house was utterly still. She took a few steps forward, listening, then instinctively, she turned round and ran to the front door. As she emerged, Martin went sprinting across the lawn to his car from the back of the house. She ran after him, kicking off her shoes as the high heels sank into the grass. He angled himself to get into the driver's seat and the engine roared into life, just as she reached the passenger door and yanked on the handle. The door opened and instantly the interior light came on. Crouched down on the passenger seat was a woman with blonde hair. Sarah froze. The car took off, slowly at first, spitting gravel against her legs, until, with a sudden wrench, it pulled her, still clinging to the door handle, after it. She felt the grinding crunch as her unprotected hip bone hit the ground, and the pain of small stones raking the entire length of her body and tearing at the side of her face. Then she let go. Her arm flopped limply to the ground and she rolled over onto the lawn.

Somehow, she got herself into the house, still dazed. The large art deco mirror in the hall confronted her with a sight she hardly recognised. Before her was a woman broken and torn. Her blonde hair was darkened on one side by mud or blood. Her face was streaked where the gravel had clawed her flesh. Her dress was ruined and her new black stockings were in shreds. Beneath the remnants of her previous lustre, was raw and bleeding flesh.

At first, numbed, she merely paced up and down the sitting room, shying away from any realisation of what had just happened. Then suddenly, she was furious. She raged out loud. She smashed a valuable figurine into the fireplace. She was about to send another one hurtling after it, when a beam of light from outside swivelled round the room. Peering through the sheer drapes at the window, she watched Martin get out of his car, slam the door and make for the house. But Sarah's attention was drawn back to the car. The passenger door had opened. The blonde woman got out, keeping her head bent and her face shrouded by hair. Slowly, she followed Martin towards the house. Already he was opening the front door. Sarah ran across the room, reaching the vestibule as he entered. She still clutched the heavy china ornament. Behind Martin was the shadowy shape of his companion. Sarah felt the arm that was clutching the figurine swing back and up to smash against this woman's face, but at the last moment, Martin caught her wrist and pinned both arms to her sides. Gently, he pushed her backwards into the hallway so that he and the woman could enter. 'What are you trying to do?' Sarah gasped. 'Calm down,' he ordered, his voice deliberate and level. 'I didn't realise you got dragged,' he continued. He indicated the woman half hidden behind him. 'Sam told me. We came back to see if you were all right.' Sarah struggled against his grip and began to weep. 'Why did you bring her here? What are you trying to do to me?' He took a deep

breath and contemplated the ceiling. 'You always make such
a fuss,' he said. 'Look.' He side-stepped so that, for the first
time, Sarah saw the woman plainly. Sarah readied her grip on
the figurine, raising her arm as much as he would allow, prepared to seize her chance if he relaxed his grip for an instant.
The woman could not have been more than sixteen or seven-
teen. She had straight, blonde hair and the delicate pink and
white complexion that only certain red or fair haired people
have. Even with her head bent, Sarah judged that she was
quite tall and slim. Her clothes were shabby. The girl glanced
up briefly with large blue eyes. She might have been her
sister. Confused, Sarah let her arm drop to her side and turned
away. But Martin held fast to her arm. Out of the corner of
her eye, she saw him reach out with one foot and gently kick
the glass-paned vestibule door so that it almost closed, leaving the girl loitering by the front door. She felt Martin bend
to catch her eye and turned away. But his head moved round
following her no matter how she twisted and turned until at
last he snared her line of sight. Holding her gaze, he brought
her head up. She looked at him, miserably, defeated and
hopeless. 'You see,' he said softly, 'she's nothing to worry
about. She's just a dumb blonde.' Involuntarily, Sarah's eyes
flicked towards the girl. It was unlikely that she could have
heard, but Sarah could have sworn she saw the girl flinch. She
looked at her for a moment. If she had been her younger
sister, she would have bought her something better than that
old jacket to wear. She turned back to Martin, straightening
to her full height so that she looked him directly in the eye.
'Then what does that make me?' she asked with a sad half-
smile. For a moment, it was his turn to be confused. She
grabbed her chance and twisted out of his grasp, stepping
back. He lunged after her, but she was already far beyond his
reach. 'Now leave.' Her voice rang with decision. He regarded her for a moment, assessing the situation, then reached
out tentatively. 'I'll call the police.' Again he looked at her
speculatively, before turning away, shaking his head in mysti-
fication.

Not until they had both gone and the sound of his car
had completely died away, did she relax. Wearily, she leant
against the wall, closing her eyes. When she opened them, she
saw herself in the mirror. One side of her face and body was
wrecked, while the other side was almost untouched. She
pushed a caked strand of hair back from her wounded cheek,
then turned her head the other way. The unsullied hair on
that side glowed blonde in the lamplight. She shook it out

and watched it shimmering. Yes, she thought. She was beginning to get used to it. It was beginning to look more like
her.

ROSA MACPHERSON

HOUSED IN A DREAM

All my life I have been devastated by everything and touched by nothing. Oh I've had my moments no doubt, like everyone else. Birth, death, suicide, even madness. Not my own you understand, but I've seen it, and read about it too. And at close quarters. But nothing has touched me. Nothing at all. I'm lucky that way.

It's a safe way to be and I recommend it entirely. It has taken a lifetime I admit, I don't want to give the impression that it's a gift or something. It's taken thousands of hours with my head shielded between the covers of some book, housed in an imaginary world. And if I've occasionally looked up from the page and witnessed an unpalatable sight, my escape has always been clear. I just look down again. Take a typical example. If the dog messes in the tulips, I can always say, 'Oh you clear that up. I've just reached an exciting part of the story.' Other people use drugs or drink to get out of things, but personally, nothing in the world beats a good read. Alright, I admit, sometimes it has not been that easy. Like the summer I discovered Hardy.

I would sit in the garden with a glass of cold beer in one hand, a cigarette in the other, couched on a wonderfully soft armchair I had bumped all the way down from the upstairs bedroom, and then I'd wallow in the bliss of the Wessex world. By the way, I recommend that *Tess of the d'Urbervilles* only be read in the warmth of the midday sun; amid the lingering scent of newly cut grass, and the twinkling of lobelia beyond the rim of the page: it adds the final touches to the scene.

As I was saying, that summer I spent in the company of Hardy. Sometimes Harry-Next-Door would loiter in his garden, over the fence, and bemoan the problems of raging weeds and persistent nettles in his fuchsias. And that was fine. Harry-Next-Door was a quiet body; alone in the world, but awfully uncomplicated and rather, well, sterile. His house was like a waiting room; no brimming ashtrays, no magazines, no dirty socks stuffed behind the cushions. He was very reliable.

I must confess, his daily-washed knickers and pillowcases flapping on the clothesline got on my nerves. His kitchen window — opened just six inches and no more, to keep the room fresh — jarred me, and I longed sometimes to go in there and fling it open, wide, just to alter his routine a bit, you understand.

Anyway, to get to the point. I had reached that part in *Tess* when she and Clare were falling in love — I could see through him, I can tell you, and he would call her 'Artemis and Demeter,' you know the bit, and she would say, 'Call me Tess' — quite right too, when suddenly I noticed that Harry's window was closed. It struck me as being so strange that I left Tess to her fate and went to investigate. As I was climbing over the fence, I noticed that the knickers on the line were the same knickers that had been gaily suspended there all week. Stranger still I thought. Well I'll tell you, when I looked throught that window and saw greasy dishes lying by the cooker and cigarettes stubbed out in the butter dish, I knew something was up.

I knocked on the door; there was no answer. Just as I was about to try the handle, I noticed the door keys still in the lock. I took them out and opened the door. 'Harry,' I said, not loud enough to be a shout I didn't want to go embarrassing myself, but loud enough for him to hear nevertheless. No answer. I tried again and it was then I saw him. He was lying on the kitchen floor with an absolutely filthy matted cover over him and he was fast asleep! I'll tell you, I just could not believe my eyes. He must have had some sort of a brainstorm. He was snoring heavily; quite disgusting I thought, and the smell! Phew, it was like a badly run brewery. Just as my eyes were taking in the astonishing sight of three empty whisky bottles lying by the bin, he woke up. Well I just didn't know where to look. But my embarrassment did not end there.

'Oh Maura,' he said, and held out his tremulous hand for me to help him.

I pretended not to notice and turned to place the keys on the wall hook.

He staggered to his feet with the help of the kitchen sink and started to mutter his apologies. It was then I had my next shock. When I looked at his face, I actually failed to recognise his features for several moments. His eyes were so altered. They were, well I suppose you would say they were full of pain, although he didn't look ill. Just so different from that blank, but friendly, safe Harry I was used to. And the growth on his face. Totally out of character. It made him look indecently wise; hard and cynical, as if he'd seen it all, you know?

I didn't like this Harry at all.

'I'm on the drink Maura,' he confessed, and I was more sympathetic when I detected a note of shame in his voice. 'I'm an alcoholic. I've been off the drink since before you moved here, but I've felt it coming on for months now, ever since Doreen died.'

Doreen was his sister; his only remaining relative. I vaguely remembered her sitting in the garden with an ice-cream cone dripping onto her skirt and her not being able to clean it on account of the stroke she had had. Harry used to move her to various points among the flowerbeds he grew specially for her; that way she could follow the sun.

That was all I remembered of Doreen.

Admittedly, I felt sorry for Harry then — even although his behaviour was against all of my principles — but he looked so pathetic. He literally was the opposite Harry from the one I knew.

Naturally I cleared up and did my best to clean him up. He let me tidy the house a bit, although he was reluctant to see the place clean, and him always so fussy too. But I did it anyway. I ignored him when he said that the place had to be dirty; I knew it was the drink talking. I was not so successful with cleaning *him* up though. He absolutely refused to have a bath and a shave. He was adamant that he could only wash when he got sober again.

'You don't have to look bad though, while you're drinking,' I said.

'Yes I do,' he answered.

Well I've never professed to understand people like that. Nevertheless, he bothered me. I had dreams at night and his face; his new face, kept breaking into focus and disturbed my rest.

I was determined to set him right though, if only to get peace again to finish off *Tess*, from the renewed comfort of my garden armchair.

It was no easy task. Whenever I raised the subject he would start on about the 'bastard Japs' and how they killed all his friends during the war. Well I'd seen 'Tenko'; I knew what he was talking about, but I didn't think it was healthy, all this talk of how a plate of stolen rice was the closest he'd ever come to heaven.

Anyway, by this time he had become quite agrophobic
so it was easy to force him to go 'cold turkey'. I bought him
beer — but no whisky. I had to keep giving him cigarettes; he
couldn't roll his own anymore. His hands flew everywhere
and his legs acted as if they wanted to dance and he didn't.
And how he talked. I don't think I had ever heard him say so
much in all the time I had known him.

'I should have married. I wish I'd married. There's no-
one left. After me, there's no-one left.'

And I thought of Tess and the d'Urberville bloodline, and
all the problems it had caused her, and I reckoned he was
well out of it.

I often wondered though, especially since he had no family left, about that name tattooed on his forearm. It said
'Patricia'. Nothing else. But I didn't like to ask him about it.

I figured that the cabinet was a safer topic of conversation, so one day when I was dusting the furniture for him,
(he still had the jitters), I mentioned how much I admired the
massive dark-wood dresser he kept in the dining-room. It almost reached the ceiling and every inch of it had been hand-
carved into little jutting diamond-shapes. It was beautiful.

'My grandfather made that,' he said. 'He carved every
piece of it himself. I remember when I was a little boy I
would watch him chisel away, and I would be mesmerised.
He made it for my grandmother; she had always wanted one.
It took him until my eighth birthday to finish it, and he told
me that one day it would belong to me and my wife. Well it
certainly is mine now, but it worries me, standing there. My
grandfather made that out of love and it should be in a happy
home. What'll happen to it when I've gone?'

It really was not such a pretty dresser close up. I spent
too much time on it I think.

But Harry got better. He gradually lost his fear of the
outdoors and when he worked on his weeds, and I was engrossed with Tess, we never spoke about that little lapse of
his. But I'll tell you, it had quite devastated me. All that
drink and dirt and shaking and all, had been some strain. I
had found it difficult to enjoy anything and for all that time,
reading was just out of the question. I had no time, for a start,
and anyway it was somehow difficult to concentrate; even
with my glass of cold beer, the cigarettes and the warm sunshine.

But then things have always come along and spoiled my
peace and quiet. Mind you, not that things have happened to

me personally, but to people I know, and I always seem to get dragged in somehow. Just like Tess.

I always seem to be in the wrong place at the wrong time, and afterwards I say 'If only I hadn't been there,' or 'if only I hadn't done this.' Take the day I met Lynne, for example. If I had only been a few minutes later, or had decided to go home through the town, instead of by the park, I wouldn't have bumped into her and it would have saved me some unpleasantness, I can tell you. But as it was, on that particular Tuesday, I spotted her walking towards me. Now that I think of it, it was not long after the Harry Carry On. Anyway, about Lynne. She was an old acquaintance of mine; I don't have many friends, but we bumped into one another occasionally. We had had our babies at the same time and that was enough for us to stop in the street and say 'Hi how are you?' I must admit I noticed that she wasn't looking herself. In fact, she looked downright awful, but you don't say those things do you? She had been quite portly; well fat, and it was such a shame she'd let herself go like that. I remember a time when she was stunningly beautiful, with golden skin and clear optimistic eyes and just perfect teeth. She made heads turn then. Now though, she had taken to dressing in a sort of flying cape which was always at least a foot behind her when she walked. It made her look a comical sight.

I knew right away when I saw her that something was terribly wrong. But then when she said that despite Sandy leaving her, she felt good and strong and ready to fight for custody of Wilma, I believed her. After all, I had seen her after that breakdown she had had about five years ago, and, compared to that time, she did look fine. Well she had lost an awful lot of weight, but then she needed to.

Although I was horrified about Sandy taking Wilma from her, I instinctively seemed to know not to show it. After all, she had probably been upset enough about the whole thing.

Anyway, we chatted politely for a while and when she was leaving she suddenly shouted over to me, 'Don't worry, I'll get her back. Sandy won't get the better of me. I'll get her back.' 'Well then, you must remember and do that,' I stammered. But her words threw me. She said it so totally out of the blue that I just knew she hadn't been listening to a word I had been saying.

I didn't think any more about it. Anyway I was totally engrossed in that feminist Marilyn French novel; you know the one, *The Women's Room*, when Lynne killed herself. It said on the jacket that 'THIS NOVEL CHANGES LIVES', and it certainly does. From that day to this I absolutely refuse to get into bed first just to warm the sheets for my man. Oh yes; now I make him do it for me.

I think I felt more betrayed than upset when she died. After all, I had been speaking to her only the week before and I had warned her, hadn't I? I had warned her not to let things get her down and she had promised. I can't deny it. I was angry at her. Bloody angry. I wanted to cry but we had visitors that day. I remember distinctly because I was embarrassed at the way I felt my mouth all twisted when I said 'Who wants tea?'

But I'll tell you, that *Women's Room* is some novel. It's all about how men destroy women and how they've got to fight back any way they can. It certainly opened my eyes and I enjoyed it, even although it had a sad ending.

I could see that Lynne had just let Sandy get the better of her. I should have let her read that book, that's what I should have done. But you always think of those things too late, don't you?

Oh, I must tell you though. After we got rid of our visitors that day, I decided to go and play badminton. I wasn't very good . . . compared to the men. It usually put me off going, but that night, I admit I was unsettled, I decided I needed to let off steam somehow. And I played so well. I slaughtered every man I played against. Jim, the coach, said, 'Maura, you're really coming on. You've finally developed that aggressive streak.'

And my nose felt all tight and I wanted to hit him.

Eventually though, after only about a week or so, my technique had really improved. And the men players found me quite a challenge I can tell you.

I decided then that I had been too hard on Sandy, Lynne's husband. I had obviously been prejudiced against him bebecause of that novel. You need to be careful about blaming people prematurely. After all it was common knowledge that Lynne had always been unstable and totally helpless without a man at her side. It was her third marriage too. It said something about her that her other husbands had left her as well. She must have been awfully difficult to live with.

One day I met her sister when I had gone to the fishmongers in the Main Street where she worked. After I had asked for three pieces of whiting, two big ones and a small one for the baby, I mentioned how sorry I was to hear about

Lynne.

'Imagine doing that over a man,' she said.

Anyway, that's by the way. Did I mention I am reading Wordsworth now? I like good poetry, and on the whole he appears to have been a very nice man. I prefer the poems like, 'The Idiot Boy' and 'Michael' where you can follow a really good story. That doesn't mean I dislike his other stuff. Well, not really. Although they're more difficult to understand I think we should be willing to put a bit more time and effort into reading, otherwise we'd miss an awful lot.

Take that 'Elegiac Stanzas' for instance. I couldn't make head nor tail of it until I found out that Wordsworth's brother had drowned; so that when he saw a picture of the stormy sea, he could appreciate it more than if his brother hadn't drowned. You see?

But in spite of that I must admit that I don't really get much enjoyment out of that kind of poetry.

But that's the only thing that puts me off Wordsworth. Apart from his too personal stuff, I think he's quite a good poet really.

MAURICE LINDSAY

GLASGOW SONNET 7: REMEMBERED SABBATHS

The bells clang to each other, street by street,
furthering distance, tossing clamour down
on the damp flagstone pavements of a town
emptied for Sunday. Cautiously discreet,
the dressed-up worshippers group in hushes; greet
like casual strangers, each as if on loan,
so couldn't be the first to cast a stone
against such managed communal deceit.
*O God, speak to our hearts that we may feel
forgiveness for our sins*, the minister prays,
while clumsily these borrowed people kneel;
but only silence meets his tremulous brays;
so up they rise on knees of suppled zeal,
reclaim their sinful selves; and nothing said.

GLASGOW SONNET 8: CURTAINS

Discarded curtains on a sale room floor,
velour, dark crimson, but the texture bare;
a dusty heap of cloth. Yet, as I stare,
I see them living, through a childhood door
I can't now enter; watch my mother pour
coffee for those around the fireside; hear
my father call for music, and an air
of Mozart's; feel my lost self ring the chore
of shutting darkness and the thickened roar
of traffic out; the inarticulate fear
of weighted menace somehow gathered there
that, should it break, must carry all before.
The wave has cast and carried; all are gone,
and thin the thread their memory hangs upon.

A BIRTHDAY CARD TO NORMAN MacCAIG
AT SEVENTY-FIVE

Old conjuror who wears no wizard's hat,
with words for fingers, images for wrists,
you juggle up the thought of *this* or *that*,
unknot delight from countless hidden twists,
manipulate a metaphysical *me*
and trick alive what's there for all to see.

DERICK THOMSON

AN t-SEALG

Tha 'm bàs a' sealg air mo chrìochan a-nis,
a' leagail companaich m'òige,
a' tighinn le a ghaiseadh
air falt liath don tug mi urram,
a' lìonadh a mhàileid
leis a' ghòraich 's leis a' ghliocas.
Bha uair a bha e sealg air a' chreachann:
tha e nis a' creachadh air a' chòmhnard.

THE HUNT

Death hunts on my territory now,
 bringing down my youthful companions,
coming with its blight
to grey-haired ones I honoured,
filling his satchel
with folly and wisdom.
Once it hunted on the scree:
now it plunders on the plain.

CEOL

Nuair a dh'fhairich mi 'n toiseach
ceòl air mo bhilean
bha an saoghal binn
's mi ri farchluais;
's an ceann greise
thainig faobhar air a' ghrinneas
's chaidh a phrìs an àird;
chan eil math a-nis
a bhith 'g iarraidh faobhar gun ghearradh
is ceòl gun bhinn,
's bho sguir mi dh'fharchluais
tha cho math a dhèanamh
mar a tha e,
geur no milis.

MUSIC

When I felt first of all
music on my lips
the world was melodious
and I eavesdropped on it;
and after a while
the elegance acquired a cutting edge
and its price went up;
it's no good now
looking for an edge that doesn't cut
and for music without sentence,
and since I stopped eavesdropping
it's as well to make it
as it is,
sharp or sweet.

RAYMOND VETTESE

THE DEID-SPALE

The deid-spale at your bedside yon nicht;
neist day we fund ye
cauld, wi een ayont licht,
an' the cannle brunt doon, its creesh
in a shool: a face thrawed wi fricht.

WILMA MURRAY

PRIVATE ENTERPRISE

Meg knelt by the pool with the sun on her back. By turning her head this way and that she hoped to spy the dimpled traces of frogspawn on the water among the weeds. She held her breath, for the smell of the water was green-sharp and strong. When she dipped her hand in to fish for the clumps of tadpole jelly, the water breathed up at her in foul bubbles and her fingers came out stinking of rotting stuff.

'Puch!' She wiped her hands on the hem of her dress, a new second-hand one from Raggy Morrison's which she refused to like even if it had saved her Mam some precious clothing coupons.

Sometimes she was seduced from the search by her own reflection. Where the water was still and the sun just right, her face was half silhouetted, half mirrored, giving her the deep dark colour of a much prettier child. She tried out various expressions on this mask, but mostly she just studied the improvement.

'I wish I was . . ' She started to speak in the whispery voice she used to herself and then stopped and looked about her.

She had patrolled half the perimeter of the pool in this way before she found any frogspawn. By that time, her knees were sore, covered in mud and inlaid with a mesh of crushed grasses and grit. Her jam-jar was half full of jelly, so she topped it up with fresh water and added some weed for good measure. In the sun her jar seemed full of little black eyes staring at her through the soupy water.

'Don't you dare die on me this year,' she told the eyes.

She walked back the way she had come, back on to the path again, nursing her jam-jar with one arm. Even walking carefully it was difficult to stop the water from slopping over. The sleeve of her cardigan was already soaked and a dirty brown stain was spreading down the front of her dress.

'Mam'll kill me.'

Just beyond a turn in the path, where it began to climb to the drive, she saw a man sitting down by the water. She

knew every man on the estate well enough to know at once
that he was a stranger. She hesitated and slowed her walk,
watching him all the time as she got nearer.

He looked hot and sweaty in a dark serge suit, even with
the trouser legs rolled up and his feet dangling in the water.
He leaned forward to examine one of his heels and she noticed
then he had a large battered suitcase on a canvas harness lying
beside him. She recognised the suitcase.

'Hullo.' She stepped up to him quite boldly then, with a
smile. 'That's Red Jean's suitcase, isn't it?'

For a moment he looked startled, squinting up at her into
the sun. 'That's right. And how do you come to know my
Jeannie?'

'She comes every year. Mam always gets her spaver buttons and safety peens from Red Jean.'

'And what do you get?'

Meg shrugged. 'Nothing usually.'

'So you live around here, then?'

'Just up the drive. Hey, do you like my tadpoles?' She
stuck the jam-jar right under his nose.

'I'd keep them out of the sun if I were you.'

'Why?'

'You'll stew the poor little devils.'

'Oh. Okay. Do you know about tadpoles? I never get
mine to hatch. And I could do with a bit of string to carry
the jam-jar home. You don't have a bit, do you?'

'I'll have a look.'

He began a search through his pockets while she set the
jam-jar down in the long grass in the bank and sat down beside the man. The skin of his feet was much whiter than his
face and where the water washed over his legs, the thick
black hair was sleeked almost to a pelt.

'You've got really hairy legs.' She studied her own by
comparison. 'Mine aren't hairy at all.'

He handed her a piece of string he had found in his pocket.
'You'll get your frock dirty sitting here.'

'It's dirty already.' She lifted her arm to show him the
stain under her arm.

'So I see.'

Her eyes slid to the suitcase. 'Where's Jean, anyway?'

'She's at home with the new bairn.'

'Another one?'

'Aye. Another one. But it's a lad this time. M.R. Simpson
& Son. That'll look good above the shop, now, won't it?'

'Do you have a shop, then?'

'Not yet. But I'm going to have, soon. Then me and Jean can stop trailing around the countryside like hawkers. Just look what it does to my feet.' He lifted a foot out of the water and showed her a blister on his heel.

'There's a notice at the end of the drive that says NO HAWKERS. Are you not a hawker, then?'

'No, no. I'm a travelling haberdasher.'

'Haberdasher?' Meg laughed. 'That's a really funny word.'

'I suppose it is. But that's what I am.'

'Have you got anything bonny in your case today?'

The man was drying his feet roughly on the grass and putting on his socks and boots. 'Oh, I'm sure I'd have something to take your fancy.'

'Any ribbons? Pink ones?'

'So that's what you're after. A ribbon for your bodice, eh?'

'Bodice? What's a bodice?'

'Oh, well, I suppose that's an old fashioned word, nowadays. For your petticoat, then?'

'I don't wear petticoats, either.' She laughed and hitched up the hem of her skirt to hook a finger into the leg elastic of a sturdy pair of green knickers. 'See?'

'Well, well. In the face of such opposition, haberdashery could just be a moribund trade.'

'You know, you talk funny. Like books.'

The man laughed. 'And you're a cure. Come on. Tie that piece of string round the neck of your jar and we'll go and see if your Mam will buy you a pink ribbon.'

'She won't. They're too dear. But you could let me have a look at them. Couldn't you? Please.'

The man considered this for a moment. 'Well. I'll make a bargain with you. If you tell me all about the folk round here, who might be needing what and that sort of thing, I'll show you the pink ribbons. Okay?'

'Oh, yes!'

Inside the case there were ribbons of every colour coiled neatly in rows among the elastic, buttons and lace. He pulled the pins from two rolls and draped the ribbons over the back of the suitcase. One was pink satin and gleamed in the sun. The other was a dark soft velvet.

'Ooh!' Meg reached out to touch them but he guided her hand away.

'Not to touch. Dirty fingers spoil ribbons.'

Meg quickly hid her hands behind her back. 'Mam'll never buy me one, though. But they're lovely. I'd put them in my hair.' She touched the untidy curls escaping from the tether of a huge metal grip. 'It's almost straight when it's washed, you know.'

'Mm. Let's go see your Mam, anyway. You never know.' He touched her lightly on the head and looked hard at her for a moment.

'What are you looking like that for?'

'Face flannels. Yes, definitely a possible investment.'

'Oh, I know I'm a mess. Mam just goes mad.'

'Not without cause, I'd imagine. Tell me, is your Mam pretty?'

'I don't know. She's okay, I suppose. Why?'

'Oh, just wondering. Come on. Let's go.'

On the way up the drive, she answered all his questions as best she could, telling him who had new bairns needing pearl buttons and narrow pastel ribbon, who was getting married and might need lace and who wouldn't buy anything at all from a man at the door. Some people, he explained, didn't know the difference between hawkers and travelling salesmen.

'What's the difference, anyway?' Meg asked.

'Ambition.'

'What does that mean?'

'Wanting to better yourself. You want to better yourself, don't you? Get on?'

'I just want to get these tadpoles to hatch.' She held the jar up to examine it once again. 'What do you know about tadpoles?'

After questioning him carefully on the care of tadpoles and young frogs, Meg bounced the hope that she might hatch out several frogs for once, instead of watching the wriggling tadpoles die and begin to stink in the scummy water which her Mam banished first to the shed and eventually to the midden.

'There's my house now.' She pointed up the path to a small low cottage among trees. 'I'll go and tell Mam you're here.'

She ran the last hundred yards to the house as quickly as she could with the jam-jar. Her mother was in the kitchen, baking.

'There's a man coming to see you. It's Red Jean's man. He's told me all about how to keep my tadpoles. Look!'

'Get those things out of here. And just look at the state of you!' She looked out of the window, watching the man approach. 'I don't think I need anything today.'

'But Mam, he's got lovely pink ribbons.'

'How would you know that?'

'We made a bargain and he showed me.'

The man was now at the back door. 'Meg. Go feed the hens and take in the eggs. They should have been done ages ago.'

'But Mam ... '

'The hens, Meg.' She patted her hair and straightened her apron before turning to the door. 'Hullo. Meg tells me your Jean's man. Well, I'm sorry you've come all the way up the drive for nothing, but I don't really need anything today.'

'Now, now. I don't believe a pretty wife like you doesn't need something for herself. A silk scarf maybe or some lace for your petticoat?' He opened his case on the doorstep.

Meg took off round the corner, not daring to linger under her mother's steady stare. Safely out of sight, she stopped to listen, however, the scoop of oats in her hand. The eager hens flapped round her feet clacking and fluttering and covering the adults' conversation. She threw handfuls of oats distractedly to try to get rid of them, but it did not work. She gave up, then, and went off to collect the eggs.

Now and again she could hear her mother laughing the giggling laugh she used when Dad was in a teasing mood. She wondered for a minute if they were laughing at her, but something in her mother's voice made her sure she was not the topic of conversation at all.

She found a legitimate excuse to go back to the house when the old Rhoddy wouldn't budge and pecked at her every time her hand came near.

'I'm just wanting the fireside shovel.' She stepped over the open suitcase lid on the doorstep. The adults stopped their talking till she was inside.

'That's a novel way to collect eggs.' Meg heard the man say.

'Oh, the shovel's just to lift up the hen's head so she can get her hand underneath.'

'I must try that with Jean sometime.'

Meg ducked past them again, laughter following her out. Her face blazed and she wished now that the man would go away and stop making her mother laugh like that.

When she came back with the scoop full of eggs at last,

the man was gone. She came in sullen and wary to find her mother looking at her in an odd way.

'Come here,' her mother said. Without warning, she delivered a hard open-handed slap to the back of Meg's legs.

'What was that for?' Meg gasped.

'That's for being so forward with a stranger. Oh, he was fair taken up with you, for some reason. What were you up to?'

'What do you mean? I haven't been up to anything.'

'You can never trust hawkers, you know.'

'He's not a hawker! He was nice to me. I liked it. And so did you!'

This time the slap was right across her face, bringing instant tears. As her head spun sideways, Meg caught sight of a little bundle of purchases lying on the kitchen table. There was a loose roll of white trimming lace, silk stockings, two cards of fancy buttons, a clutch of safety pins and a hairbrush. There was no pink ribbon.

Meg swung her head back round to glare at her mother, accusingly. Her mother turned away.

'Oh, I know,' she said. 'But I did only use the egg money.' She fingered the lace on the table without enthusiasm. 'Anyway, best not tell your Dad, eh? And here, you better have this.' Slowly, she pulled a length of pink ribbon from her apron pocket.

'He left it for you.'

PAT GERBER

TO SLEEP, PERCHANCE

'And they all lived happily ever after.' Meg closed the book and sighed. Why did she tell these lies to her daughter after what had happened to her, to them? Her mouth uttered the pleasing words but her mind was semi-frozen into a state of slow-action replay, her being in schism.

'Don't leave me yet Mummy,' the child's eyes held her. 'Tell me just one more. Tell Daddy's one. Please?'

Two hours had passed since 'Daddy' had left. Although she'd soon be going to school, Dawn still liked being read to and the old fairy-tales she knew almost by heart were the stories she preferred. Since Dawn was no more than a baby, Meg and 'Daddy' had read her a nightly story apiece.

'Sorry love. I've got work to prepare for classes tomorrow.' Apologising, always inadequate to meet the demands made on her by others. Perhaps tonight extra pains were needed. 'Which story love?'

'The Sleeping Beauty. Because of going to the ballet tomorrow.'

The book was old and grey, the paper rough-edged, flannel-thick. They'd found it in a junk-shop in Penzance, long before Dawn had come along to prove their union. Page forty. Meg's age. Life was supposed to begin now, not end.

The illustrations were like misty memories of past pantomimes. At the beginning pink, blue and bronze courtiers followed a golden coach through autumn trees. She read out the caption. 'All the company returned to the Royal Palace to find a great feast arranged.'

For some reason she remembered their wedding, the billowing white dress that had lied about her purity, the stiffly formal hotel meal, the sense of escape afterwards.

Dawn had turned to the next picture. Gentle pinks, rose-brown, soft green, the princess asleep with two cherubs skipping through a cloud of golden mist and the prince looking at her, his hand on his heart. 'He beheld the loveliest vision he had ever seen.'

He had once called her his princess. In these days she too

had believed you really could live happily ever after once you were wed. She knew better now.

'Read, Mummy.' Dawn knew the ritual. First the pictures, then the story, then the goodnight kiss. So little to make the child feel secure, safe in Meg's affections.

'Once upon a time there lived a King and a Queen, who lacked but one thing on earth to make them entirely happy.'

She knew how they'd felt, Meg thought. Married twelve years and his parents always on at you about the joys of a family. They never thought about the problems, the responsibilities. She'd stuck to her principles. Until they could do without her salary, she'd stay on the pill.

Eventually, as he became bored with her, she gave in. Perhaps a child would bring them together again, a son to carry on the name, a sop to tradition. But after the barren years of tests and trials she'd given up.

She'd make her mark through work. When she'd won her first promotion she'd begun to feel sick in the mornings. It had not been some germ, it had turned out to be Dawn. Aged thirty-five, she'd had to rethink her life completely.

He'd gone off her pregnant body. Disappointed that she hadn't brought forth a son, he took time to accept Dawn so Meg had started calling him 'Daddy' to make him feel a part of things.

She'd gone back to work. First there had been the au pair girls, but 'Daddy' of the increasing paunch and the roving eye had made life impossible for them. One after the other they'd left in disgust. Now Dawn went to a childminder like the children of other lecturers.

Meg dragged her mind back to what she was reading. 'They invited all the fairies they could find in the land to be godmothers to the Princess Aurora, that each one of them might bring her a gift.' Meg loved Quiller-Couch's slow rolling style.

'Tell me about my christening, Mummy.'

Meg shook her head. 'Not tonight darling.' But as she read on mechanically Dawn's baptism drifted into her mind. Even then, 'Daddy' had been chasing one of her friends.

Why had it always been someone she knew? Of course if there were others she'd not have found out. As it was, someone always felt the need to inform her, usually after the affaire was over, for her own good.

Her friends — there had been eight in the bunch — would tell her of the times 'Daddy' had made passes at them. They'd laugh with her at his stupidity, his arrogance in thinking they'd play with her partner. One, Zilla, had talked many times with Meg, advising her sympathetically.

Dawn interrupted her thoughts. 'Tell about the wicked fairy.'

'Seats of honour had been set for the seven fairy god-mothers — '

'Auntie Zilla was my fairy godmother.'

Godmother. What an irony, Meg thought.

'Will Auntie Zilla be my — my spare mummy now?'

Too tired for the inevitable question and answer session, Meg continued reading. 'To the dismay of everyone there appeared in the doorway an old crone, dressed in black and leaning on a crutched stick. Her chin and her hooked nose almost met together, like a pair of nutcrackers. She growled to the guests in a terrible voice "I am the Fairy Uglyane!" '

If only Zilla had been ugly, or fat, or even faithful. If only she could have seen into Zilla's mind. How was it that she'd never suspected? She must have been as credulous as this child who believed in fairies. 'One of the younger fairies, Hippolyta by name, overheard her mumbling threats between her teeth and hid herself close by the cradle behind the tap-estry so that she might have the last word and undo, so far as she could, what evil the Fairy Uglyane might have in her mind.'

'Evil, weevil, weevil evil,' intoned Dawn, beginning to get sleepy at last.

Meg read through the list of virtues bestowed on the Princess Aurora and thought how the needs of women had changed since the story was written. Beauty and wit were still useful, but you needed much more than the abilities to dance, sing and 'play exquisitely on all instruments of music'. There was so much you had to cope with, Today's ideal woman was expected to be a success in her career, materially wealthy, perfectly packaged for marriage, sexy and maternal. See Dynasty for the fairy tale of today.

' "This is my gift to you, Princess Aurora," announced the hag, in her creaking voice that shook as spitefully as her body. "One day you shall pierce your hand with a spindle, and on that day you shall surely die!" ' Meg looked at her sleepy daughter and wondered how the events of today would affect her in the future. She didn't feel capable of being a single parent. 'The fair Hippolyta stepped forth from behind the tapestry saying "Your daughter shall not die thus. She must indeed pierce her hand with a spindle, but instead of dying, she shall only fall into a deep slumber that shall last for many years, at the end of which a King's son shall come and wake her.'

Soon Dawn would be asleep. Then she, Meg, would have to face alone the events of this day. Softening her voice, she read on. Anything to stave off the unbelievable facts. 'After the wicked witch had taken her departure, riding away, it was generally agreed, upon a broomstick, the palace fireworks were duly set off.'

Dawn mumbled 'We had fireworks at Auntie Zilla's party. I didn't like the bangs. Daddy was brave.'

Where will you go? Meg had asked 'Daddy'. To Zilla's?

I've taken a room, 'Daddy' had said, till the divorce is through. It will be less awkward for Zilla and the children.

Less awkward? She hadn't actually believed this conversation was taking place, so her voice had sounded quite normal, as in discussing the neighbour's cat.

Teenagers you know. Zilla feels it would be difficult for them to explain to their friends.

Of course, she had replied conversationally. It wouldn't just be easier for you to stay on here till you —

No.

So keen to escape, to break their tie. So anxious for Zilla's peace of mind.

'Go on Mummy. You've stopped.' Dawn snuggled deeper under the duvet. So confident in Meg's care, so seemingly secure. Would she be alright, without 'Daddy'? Broken families were blamed for delinquency, truancy, even drug-addiction these days. Meg herself had been known to explain away a difficult student, Oh he comes from a broken home, that's the cause.

She read on, doggedly. 'The King drew up a proclamation that forbade everyone, on pain of death, to use a spindle.' Pain of death. Would death be worse than what was to come for her, for Dawn?

The child's breathing was deepening. Meg paraphrased the story a little, about how the spindle pierced the princess's finger and made her swoon. 'And the King came galloping home to the Palace. He gave orders to carry the Princess to the finest apartment and there lay her on a bed embroidered with gold and silver.'

Would 'Daddy' gallop home in his white hatchback and help out in a crisis? What would happen if she got ill, couldn't cope? Childish weakness swept over Meg for an instant, but she dammed it back.

She forced her mind onto the task in hand. 'The King sent for the good fairy Hippolyta who, in an hour, arrived at the Palace in a fiery chariot drawn by dragons.'

Veronica in her Porsche, Meg thought, irrelevantly. Later tonight she could phone Veronica, tell her 'Daddy' had finally gone. Then she might begin to believe the impossible truth of it herself.

'Hippolyta approved of all the King had done, but greatly foreseeing, she touched with her wand everything and everybody in the Palace. That very instant they all fell asleep.'

There was no escaping the fact that she was now reading to a sleeping child. To sleep, perchance to dream. Meg's thoughts began to drift more wildly. There were the sleeping tablets. People committed suicide in situations like this. But it seemed, somehow, too dramatic a gesture for her to make. Anyway she lacked the courage.

And Dawn. She would now be more or less without a father. She'd need Meg in double strength, not dead.

Anyway, to do away with one's whole life for one rotten man could be to over-react. Other people had survived divorce. Maybe she would. It was just that at this moment she lacked self-confidence and other necessary strengths.

It wasn't that 'Daddy' had beaten her. Just that he could not resist other women, and didn't appear to try. She had become abject in her efforts to please him. Guilt riddled her like woodworm. Magazine agony aunts told her that her man strayed because something was wrong at home. In other words she was useless in bed. But her brain told her that, on the contrary, perhaps there was something wrong with 'Daddy'. Counsellors suggested she ride out the storm and it would all blow over. How many women constituted a storm?

When the known count reached a dozen, Meg's patience had run out. With her self-esteem at zero, she'd indulged in a meaningless affaire herself. It had boosted her ego — and increased her guilt.

The confusing thing was that illogically she still loved 'Daddy'. She loved his sunny nature, devoid as he was of all introspection, even though it had meant that he was incapable of talking through problems with her. He simply denied their existence. She tenderly loved every detail of him, the way his hair curled on his neck, his strong hands. Part of her wanted desperately to feel secure in his ability to take care of things as her father had always done. But he wouldn't play the role.

It was Zilla she hated, with green vitriolic loathing. For four years Zilla had been carrying on a double life with 'Daddy' that would have defied the detection methods of MI5. Not that Meg had been the least suspicious.

Quite accidentally one day when she'd been feeling bitchy she'd remarked casually, Who's the current fancy then? And he'd replied, Zilla. I thought you knew.

Of course, she had lied. Thought you'd have gone off her by now. And her mind had clamped shut while her voice went on, calm as ice, asking about Zilla, for all the world as if she were chatting to a stranger at a party. Apparently Zilla needed him, she was the helpless type, not capable like Meg.

Only later, when her mind defrosted in a scarlet heat of embarrassment, anguish and fury, did she begin to remember all the times she'd confided in her 'friend' Zilla. Her confessions about 'Daddy's' infidelities, and what they were doing to her, given freely over a stream of coffee cups and wine-glasses. Zilla had listened, and listened.

Now Meg imagined Zilla as a huge red ear drinking in every vital clue about 'Daddy'.

'Mummy you've stopped.' Dawn's eyes prised open. 'Finish my story?'

'Within a few hours there grew up around the Palace such a tangle of briars and undergrowth that neither man nor beast could find a passage. The Princess would sleep with no fears of visits from the inquisitive — ' Meg's voice droned onto automatic pilot again.

Never again would she believe anything a man said to her. Men were beasts. You couldn't trust women either, come to that.

'Daddy' had gone. The actual going had been so clear, so final, and yet so utterly unbelievable.

He had come home from the office, packed a case, taken the lamp from his side of the bed, his pillow, his book, his clock, a few photographs from the bedside drawer, and put them in the car.

Do you mind if I take the ship painting? he had asked in his everyday voice.

How could she mind? He had bought it.

And a couple of plates and things?

He had to eat. She noticed, with an empty feeling, how pale and drawn he looked.

Help yourself, she had said evenly. Would you like —
the meal's ready — before you go?

No.

He had gone then, through the front door, the cord from
his shaver trailing like some torn umbilicus, the old washbag
he'd had at boarding-school clutched to his chest like a teddy.

Won't you kiss me goodbye? She had accompanied him
as far as the door, not wanting to embarrass him, keeping her
dignity, offering her cheek.

I think not. He had walked on.

She saw the quick glance he gave the neighbouring windows as he shoved his gear awkwardly into the hatchback.
Then he was starting the engine. For an instant the farcical
nature of the situation threatened to engulf Meg in hysterical
giggles. She pinched her mouth shut.

She had waved, not waving but drowning, she had thought,
as he drove away down the road and merged into the con-
fusion of traffic.

For a long time she had stood completely numb. Like
Lot's wife, a pillar of salt. Too dry for tears, a huge lump of
indigestible agony inside her.

The child's voice had scratched her consciousness like
thorns, needling her with insistence.

Now she was almost asleep. As soon as the demanding
child-mind was switched off for the night Meg would be
alone, without defence. The realisation that she would probably be alone for a long time bled into her brain and she
could no longer stem it.

She began to examine how she felt. To her surprise there
came the merest trickle of relief. The cut was clean. The un-
certainty was over. She had come through some sort of tunnel,
now she was at the end of it. In front of her lay the rest of
her life and she was free to choose what to do with it.

Knifing through the pain of loss came the knowledge that
endless possibilities lay ahead. She could paint the whole flat
pink if she felt like it, she could laze undisturbed in bed,
spend holidays in Mull instead of Corfu, join the S.D.P. without ruining anyone's career.

And tonight? She'd phone Veronica, make a date to tell
her everything then relax with a book by the fire. No more
would heavy sighs pull at her guilt-complexes, make her run
to switch T.V. channels, fetch snacks to bribe 'Daddy' to stay
at home. He'd gone. It was too late. She'd tried her best —
and failed.

There was now this child, like a lead weight dragging her down. No, more like an anchor to keep Meg steady. She must help the child grow strong, able to take the knocks in life without the need to lean on other fragile humans.

Gently stroking her daughter's hair, she read softly on about Prince Florimond, who'd come hunting in the forest many years later, thrusting his sword into the tangled briars and magically finding a pathway through them to the sleeping Palace.

'He climbed the grand staircase and found the most beautiful Princess lying fast asleep on a bed. He fell in love with her at first sight and sank to his knees to kiss her hand that lay, light as a rose leaf, on the coverlet.'

'Mummy?' Dawn rolled over.

'Shsh — it's nearly finished. 'They were married then and there and lived — '

'What's for breakfast?'

'Porridge.' Thank goodness for the realities of everyday, thought Meg, tucking the duvet round the little pink cheek. She must work to make a good life for this child, and for herself.

She riffled through the old book. Not lies, she decided, but fantasy. A way of making life more bearable? An attempt to understand the incomprehensible sadnesses we each have to survive?

Today was nearly over. Idly she turned to the next story. It was Bluebeard. Once upon a time — . She shut the book. Tomorrow would begin soon enough.

ENID GAULDIE

A GAME OF BONES

It was the lads at the dominoes that started the crack that night in February, when the sleet was fair belting down outside and the North Sea was flinging whole water over the harbour wall and the windows of the pub were streaming wet with the congealed foul breath of the crowd inside. They had the evening paper on the table beside them and the harbour master, who was a bittie quicker brained than the most of them, was reading out bits that took his fancy as he waited his turn at the bones.

Vandalism was the topic of the night, not for the first time. The table was divided between those who claimed laddies were no worse than they'd ever been and who dearly liked to tell of the terrible crimes of their own childhood and those who believed the young had sunk to a new degree of wickedness.

'It's a good belting they're needing' was a fairly generally held view.

Brandon is a hard, grey village, set on a hard, grey coast. It is a safe haven only by comparison with the rest of the coast line which is rocky and dangerous for twenty miles on either side. A thin strip of land lies between sea and steeply rising cliffs and on that strip charmless two storey houses stare into each other's front rooms, windowless gable ends towards the sea. No pretty cottages clustering here, this place was built in the short, greedy, graceless time when there was big money to be made out of herring. The herring gone, there is a living left at the lines but there are only a few boats left now where once there were scores of them.

Harbour repairs have sklerried over the old red stone piers with dulled, grey concrete. Even the scouring sea has a soiled fringe of electric blue plastic bleach bottles and foil carry-out cartons tangling with cast seaweed and strips of old carpet. In the 1950s an improving county council sited a block of public lavatories at the foot of the pier road, between the houses and the sea.

There is a mission hall, but no church. Folk here have

never been greatly taken with ministers. They keep their respect for the sea and give none of it to man. For them the sea is the visible arm of their own terrible god and they have more sense than not to fear it.

The village has two public houses. One of them sits down at the harbour and is the accustomed meeting place of fisher men, a decent enough place so far spared the attentions of shop fitters and interior designers. The other is barely worth attention. It has been brought up to date with formica tables and a juke box and is, in any case, frequented by folk from the cottar houses and such like trash.

Up to a point this is a matriarchal society and a grown man will be known as Maggie Jean's James or Mary Bella's Thomas to the end of his days. But the women keep indoors. For an hour in the morning you might see them about the street, in their wrap-around flowered pinnies and baffies trimmed with mauve fur on their bunioned feet. They shuffle off to the shoppie to get something to their man's tea and they stop here and there for a crack with a wifie dashing her hearth rug at the door or another hanging out her washing at the head of the beach. It can take a fair time to buy a bone for broth, a tin of polish and a piecy cheese but when the shopping is done it will be indoors again for most of them and a day spent getting a shine on the lino.

Men are out at all times of day, young ones considering their prospects and old ones waiting for them to trip. A fair number of men too old to go to the lines attends the coming and going of the tides, inspects and criticises each day's catch and then subsides on the concrete benches at the pier's head for a pipe of tobacco. When the light fades they make their way to the Harbour Bar to sit in the darkest corner filling the air with smoke and their own harsh view of life.

Folk here are no more a pattern of neighbourly goodness than the village is picturesque. Their chief entertainment is the recounting of anecdotes showing up their friends and relations in the worst possible light. They enjoy other people's discomfiture more than anything else and they enjoy it with an unashamed simple pleasure.

Babies and toddlers are doted on, dandled and fondled and fed unsuitable, sweet, placatory tributes. Every one in the place will put a silver coin on a new baby's pram pillow or stuff lollies into an infant's fist. But once infancy is past indulgence ends. Children learn to dodge a kind of rough teasing that is more like torture and to deal each other the

same meanness, the same pinching and kicking and hair pulling that they learned at father's knee. Mothers and grand-
mothers, aunts and cousins subscribe to the same cruel dis-
cipline that the men folk administer.

'Did ye get a hiding then laddie?' they will laugh, if a
greeting youngster comes seeking sympathy. 'Dae ye want
anither?'

This is no place to come looking for soft, easy kindness.
If you are not one of us you're nothing, no good trash from
god knows where. If you are one of us you should keep your
place. Lift your head above the rest and get it smashed down.
A sour philosophy? Aye, it's sour, and this is a sour place, as
sour as all the other fisher places reckoned so couthy by
those who know nothing of them.

The Harbour Bar on a Friday night has its regulars. Creelie
sits at the far end of the mahogany bar where he can see who
comes in and assess his chance of a free pint. He has no hope
from his contemporaries but the young lads, with their curly
hair, gold ear-rings and tight breeks, include him in a round
sometimes when they are flashing money about. Creelie got
his name on an ill occasion long ago when he caught the
button of his jacket in the mesh of a lobster creel just as he
was about to cast it overboard and over he went with it into
the water. People here never let go the tail of humiliation.
They like to twitch it again when the need arises. So as
Creelie he'll go to his grave.

Jenny Christie's Jock takes the far end of the bar for
another reason. He has a scar down the side of his face he got
scaling the cliffs for gulls' eggs when he was a laddie. Not that
he fell. It was the mistress from the big house up by did it.
She caught him coming off the cliff with the eggs in his
pouch. A terrible woman for birds she was and she had warned
the boys not to go raiding nests. A woman with a temper
like that should never be let loose. She took her walking stick
and hit Jockie, right across the face, cut his face open. If it
had had a stitch it might have healed better but his mother
never held with doctors. It is a kind of an ugly, puckered,
purplish cheek right enough and he likes to sit with it turned
to the wall.

The domino school is a biling of old men that takes the
table in the middle of the public bar. That night they were on
about law and order.

'Flogging' they agreed 'flogging's what they need. Make a
public spectacle of them.'

With the terrible relish of old men contemplating the punishment of the young they savoured the thought quietly for a bit, each with his own mental picture of some coorse laddie strung up at the pier for a public flogging. Creelie, who had left his usual place to stand by and join in the talk, dribbled a little.

Then a daft young loon that should have known better than stick his oar where it wasn't needed put up the notion that punishment never did any good.

'Violence only breeds violence' he said, obviously parroting.

'Must've been watching Panorama or some daft like shite' they sneered.

'A good belting never hurt anyone' they chorused. 'Many's the belting us yins has had, eh lads', complacently.

Jockie got up from his stool at the bar, quite suddenly, and dragged in a chair to sit beside them.

'D'ye think I wis the better o this then?' he asked, putting his hand up to the scar on his face. They were taken aback, for Jockie never spoke of the incident. It had always been taken for granted that the shame of being hit by a woman had struck him dumb. But after a moment one of the bones players giggled nervously and they all joined in.

'It learned you no to harry gulls' nests though!'

They chuckled over that as they played another round, clicking the pieces into place, pairs of dots to pairs of dots, with their crooked, rheumaticky, black-nailed fingers.

'Na, na,' they said, with satisfaction, 'It's a good hiding the maist o them need. When we wis their age we had the fear o death pit intae us.'

'And nane the waur o it.'

'If it wisna the dominie it wis yer ain da and mither, or onybody else that catched ye.'

'They'd all tak a strap tae ye, soon as look at ye.'

'A right hard lot they were. Ye got off wi nothing. They wis a down on ye. The lot o them. Ye'd naebody tae rin tae.'

'Nane o yer *do-gooders* then.'

'Loons were kept down.'

'And a guid thing too.'

'Nane o us ony the waur o it.'

'Aye, aye!' the chorus line again. 'Spare the rod and spoil the child. They had the right way o it in those days.'

There was a silence, one of those moments of silence that falls on the busiest pub once in a while. The wind and the sea crashed together outside. Somebody belched. The dominoes clicked together and smacked against the table top. The bar man ran water over glasses and threw an empty, with a suddenly startling crash, into a box below the counter.

Jockie puffed his pipe, bubbling gently.

'Dae ye mind,' he said, very quietly into the silence, 'Dae ye mind when we wis laddies?'

'Fine I mind,' said one.

'Aye, we mind well enough,' said another.

'Dae ye mind, though,' said Jockie, then paused as if wondering whether to go on. The pause had the effect of making them look up for a moment from their piles of smooth, spotted bones, giving Jockie the benefit of a dozen little hard black eyes gazing from a network of deep, rusted, crows' feet. Jockie went on, as if decided on the need.

'Dae ye mind about Andra Gall, though? Dae ye mind o him?'

The noise in the bar had started up again and the new silence that fell upon the old domino players went unnoticed outside their own circle. Then one among them spoke, with an authority vested in him by the nervy quietness of the others.

'That's best forgotten.'

It was meant to be final. But something had got into Jockie that night. A kind of recklessness.

'It's been forgotten fifty years. Fifty years! Is that not long enough?'

'It's all forgotten. All in the past.'

'Aye, aye. It's past. But there's nane o us forgotten it.' Jockie turned suddenly upon his neighbour.

'Have *you* pit it out of mind?' And then, swinging fiercely in his chair, his lurid face turned to his other neighbour, 'Or you? Have *you* forgotten? Or *you*?' jabbing his pipe stem at one after the other. 'Or you? Or you? Or *you*?'

Then, almost triumphantly, he watched a creep of flushed misery on their old faces.

'Fifty years and there's nivir a one o us ever forgotten. Nivir spoke of it frae that day to this, nivir told the truth o it to onybody. Eh? Is that no the size o the thing?'

'Aye, it wis a bad business.'

'A bad business, right enough.'

'We wis jist laddies. We kent nae better.'

'Right' said Jockie. 'That's the way of it. We'd been learned our lessons, had we not? We had yer fear of death that ye speak o, we had that, the fear of death right enough. But we

kent nae better.'
'He jist fell, though. We nivir pushed him.'
'It wis an accident.'
'We couldna help it.'
Old men using children's excuses with the words left un-
spoken fifty years ago.
'He'd been tellt tae keep back fae the edge o the pier.'
'We'd a been tellt and tellt.'
'Ye canna keep laddies aff a pier's edge.'
'But he *had* been tellt. Over and over.'
Jockie let them go on for a while. Then he said, as if giving
a boulder another push down hill:
'There was nobody ever liked him.'
They looked shocked. At the time of the taking of the
boy's body from the slimy harbour water, at the funeral ser-
vice, in the weeks to come at school and home. they had
heard adult talk about a young life lost in its innocence, a
loved one gone from the community. They had forgotten,
or had buried deep the truth that nobody liked the lad, that
he was a twisted little liar, a jessie, half Sassenach, and illegi-
timate at that.
'It wis him that started the fight.'
'It wis aye him that started a punch up.'
'If he hadna run ... '
'If he hadna tripped up on yon bittie rope ... '
'If Willie hadna pit oot his foot ... '
Another moment of shocked silence fell as another icicle
of truth splintered off.
Willie spoke up as quickly as a nine year old. 'I never. I
never pit oot ma fut.'
Jockie had become a recording angel, although he made
no attempt to shoulder off his share of guilt.
'Abody kens whose foot it wis he tripped owre at the end.
But there's nivir a one o us didna gie him a shove. He wis rin-
ning fae the lot o us,'
'Right enough. We were right wee divils that day. I dinna
ken whit got intae us.'
'We were nae different that day,' said Jockie, 'from ony
ither day. But that day we didna get off wi it.'
They looked puzzled. Creelie said 'Aye but we did get
off. We wis niver catched. Naebody kent we'd ever been
there.'
Another spoke up, voicing a kind of pride they all felt.
'Not one of us ever opened his mouth. We niver tellt. We

kept mum.'

That's the right way of it,' said Jockie, as if he was coming to an important kind of truth .'We saw the laddie fall into the sea, and what did we do?'

They almost chuckled.

'We ran! By God we ran!'

'We were aff that pier and away up the cliffs before you could say Jack Robinson.'

'Aye,' said Jockie, 'We ran so fast not a soul saw us go. But why did we run?'

'We were feared.'

'We'd have got a right good hiding.'

'If they'd ha kent we'd been there when he fell ... '

'We'd fairly have got a belting.'

'My faither wud ha killed me.'

'We had the fear o death on us.'

'Aye, aye' said Jockie, 'so we did, so we did. And we let the laddie drown, we were so feared o what we'd get.'

The silence again, the fidgety silence.

'We didna think he'd fa tae his death — we thocht he'd jist get a drookin.'

'Did we?' said Jockie. 'Dae ye not think, mebbe, if we'd ha raised the alarm, if we'd ha shouted for help, if we'd rin for our faithers, we might ha got him dragged oot alive?'

'But then we'd have had to tell ... '

'They'd ha kent how it cam aboot ... '

'That's right. We'd all have got ane of they beltings you're sae keen on, would we not?'

He got up, awkwardly, steadying himself against the edge of the table.

'But the laddie Andra wud hae been alive tae play at the bones.'

Jockie walked out of the pub. He climbed up the hill to his cottage, packed his bag and caught the bus. He was away to stay with his married sister, away up the Howe, away for good, not all that sorry to be leaving Brandon behind him, even after all these years.

JANET CAIRD

FOSSILS

The shabby bull-nosed Morris Cowley turned from the main road on to the narrow track that led to Steadens. From the back seat Robert could see the house standing up against the skyline, square and bleak, and beside it the black farm buildings. He wriggled restlessly, uncomfortable in his best clothes — flannel suit, a clean white shirt, tie. Even with the air rushing past the open car, he was hot under the August sun; and if he put his hand on the mock-leather upholstery it felt burning hot. He glanced at his cousin Catherine beside him, envying her her loose white dress and the white sandals she wore. She had taken off her hat, tired of holding it on, and her fair hair was blowing back from her face. She didn't look as if she was hot and prickly, but he could see she was in a bad mood. So he said nothing. She could be very snappy when she was in a bad mood. All the same, having her to share the holiday had been, on the whole, agreeable. She was old of course — past sixteen — and he was only ten, but nevertheless they were friends; went walks together, shared the chores such as gathering eggs and feeding the hens; poled the leaky old punt on the river; swam in the murky water. And he had learned to keep out of her way when she turned moody and lay in the house reading.

She broke her sulky silence.

'Is that the house?'

'Yes.'

'What will we do there?'

'Well, we'll have tea. Mrs Wilkie always gives us a very good tea, with cream puffs and plums and junket and cream.'

'You're a greedy boy, Robert. Is that all we do?'

'We'll probably play a game with Mr Wilkie — a kind of billiards.'

'Don't they have children?'

'No.'

'Will there be any young people there?'

'No. Just us.'

'It sounds awful. I wish I wasn't going — '

Robert's mother, in the front seat, overheard her niece and said over her shoulder:

'It's very kind of Mrs Wilkie to ask us. She does it every summer. She and Mr Wilkie are fond of young people and you're to behave and not sulk.'

Her other aunt Jean who was driving said:

'You'll quite enjoy it Catherine. Robert doesn't mind it, do you Robert? And if you ask Mr Wilkie, he'll show you his fossils.'

'Fossils?'

Catherine looked at Robert.

'Mr Wilkie has boxes of fossils he's found around here. Fossils,' said Robert importantly, 'are animals that lived thousands of years ago and died and turned into stone.'

'I know what fossils are, silly.' She dropped her voice to a whisper. 'It's people like me I want to see, not fossils — or little boys.'

She made a face at Robert which he ignored.

They were now drawing up at the garden gate and Mrs Wilkie was coming down the path to greet them. Robert braced himself for an ordeal to come. Mrs Wilkie would, he knew, kiss him in greeting, as she kissed his mother and aunt and doubtless would Catherine also. Perhaps if he stretched his arm out at full length and turned his head and hung back — but it was no use. Mrs Wilkie pulled him firmly on to her unyielding bosom and kissed him heartily.

'What a big boy you've grown, Robert!'

Well, if he was a big boy, she should know better than to kiss him. Kissing was for little boys — very little boys. He gave her a less than cordial look, caught his mother's eye and managed a reluctant smile. He saw Catherine was laughing at him and almost put his tongue out at her.

They moved into the garden. This was part of the ritual: a walk round the garden, then tea, then the game, then the fossils. Catherine and Robert lingered behind the three ladies and walked sedately up the brick-laid path. It was a very neat garden, divided into rectangles, each with its vegetables — peas, scarlet runners, cabbages, cauliflower; very different from the garden at aunt Jean's farm where the flowers and vegetables were not always separate and the net over the strawberries had holes that let in the blackbirds.

They were beside a plum tree trained against the garden wall, and hung with ripe Victoria plums. Catherine stretched up and plucked one.

'Don't.' Robert was alarmed.

'Why not?'

'It's . . . We're not allowed to.'

'Who said so?'

She picked another one and offered it to him. He took it of course, enjoying both its juicy savour and the guilt. Catherine took another for herself and said:

'You didn't tell me Mrs Wilkie was very old-fashioned.'

'Old-fashioned?'

'Oh you wouldn't notice, being just a little boy. Look how she's dressed.'

Robert looked. Mrs Wilkie's dress was different from his mother's and aunt's. Her skirts were longer, much longer, and her dress had a funny high lace collar that came right up under her chin. Her hair was different too — piled up in a big knob on the very top of her head.

'Well?' said Catherine.

'I see her dress is different. And her hair . . . '

'She's wearing it the way aunt Jean has hers in her wedding photo. If you ask me, Mrs Wilkie has got frozen in time.'

Robert did not understand this. A voice behind them saved him from having to admit it.

'Hullo Robert,' said Mr Wilkie. 'I'm glad to see you. Is this young lady your cousin Catherine? How do-you-do.'

As they shook hands he said:

'I see you've found the plum tree. Take as many as you like.'

'There,' said Catherine, 'I knew it would be all right about the plums. Mr Wilkie's nice. He's much younger than Mrs Wilkie. Or didn't you notice that either?'

'I didn't need to notice. I knew.'

'How?'

'How what?'

'How did you know? That Mrs Wilkie was older than Mr Wilkie?'

'I heard them' (he nodded towards his mother and aunt) 'talking.' He was smarting under her air of superiority. 'You don't know everything. I know a lot about the Wilkies.'

'Tell me.'

'Why should I? You're always sneering at me.'

'No I'm not. Do tell me. I won't be cross ever again.'

He knew this was a blatant lie, but when Catherine was nice and her voice was soft and gentle, he liked her very much. So he said:

'Well, Mr Wilkie's mother didn't want him to be a farmer, so he went to London to learn to be a draper. But Mr Wilkie hated it and turned ill and came back. But when he was in London he married the lady where he lodged. That's Mrs Wilkie and she's fifteen years older than he is.'

'She must be *ancient*,' said Catherine. 'Poor Mr Wilkie.'

'Why "poor Mr Wilkie"?'

'Well, she looks staid and dull. I bet she never laughs or goes on picnics, or — or — '

'They say she keeps house beautifully. And that's true. It's the cleanest house I've ever been in. But she takes nothing to do with the farm — not even the hens. She's a super baker — she makes lovely cream puffs.'

'There's more to life than cream puffs, only you're so greedy I don't suppose you understand that.'

Robert didn't answer. So much for promises never to be cross again!

The others had turned and were moving towards them. Soon they were all entering the house, into the dark cool hall, all the darker for the dazzle of sun outside. Robert's eyes soon cleared and yet once more he was struck by the rigid orderliness. The polished floor gleamed, every rug was straight; on one side a door opened to the dining-room, on the other side to the sitting-room which Mrs Wilkie called the drawing-room. On either side of these doors stood upright chairs with circular seats and long narrow tapering backs all covered with squiggly designs of flowers and fruit. Robert had been told they were 'poker-work' and had been done by Mrs Wilkie's mother when she 'was only twelve'. Mrs Wilkie saw Catherine looking at them and said:

'My mother did that poker-work when she was only twelve. I'm sure you couldn't do that could you?'

She turned to answer a remark of Robert's mother; so only he heard Catherine mutter:

'I shouldn't try. They're hideous.'

They sat in the sitting-room while Mrs Wilkie made tea. It was like no other room Catherine had ever seen. Everything that could be polished shone; the mirror was spotless; the hanging crystal ornaments on the mantelpiece sparkled like newly formed icicles. The pink of the velvet upholstery and fat satin cushions of the settee and chairs were repeated in the pink roses of the carpet. On little tables scattered round the room was a variety of ornaments — a blue glass box, frilly china figures, little jugs. On the walls were pictures in narrow gilt frames — ladies in crinolines looking out of a window, a Venetian scene with a gondola, a bluebell wood of beeches. The room's immaculate neatness made her feel ill at ease and when Robert whispered:

'Did you ever see such a tidy room?' she hissed back:

'It's horrid. It's all Mrs Wilkie. You would never guess there was a Mr Wilkie from this room. I thought you said he had fossils?'

'He has. But they're kept in the wash-house.'

They moved into the dining-room, also gleaming and polished, but sombrely functional, with a long solid table, mahogany chairs with green leather seats. The clock was black marble and on the mantel-piece were little statues of rearing bronze horses. The carpet was red, the paper mid-green. In this subdued setting the tea-table was an oasis of lightness: rosebud china on a starched damask cloth; a silver tea-kettle poised above a little blue flame; a huge velvet cover over a large silver tea-pot, plates of thin bread and butter; crystal jam dishes shining like jewels; jam sponges; plum-cake, and huge cream-puffs.

Mrs Wilkie made her usual little joke; 'We'll let the men sit together' and Robert was placed beside Mr Wilkie, at an agreeable distance from his mother so that he could enjoy unchecked the good things with which Mr Wilkie plied his plate. The meal was rounded off with bottled plums, junket and cream. Mrs Wilkie might be older than Mr Wilkie, thought Robert, but she could make a jolly good tea. And what was all the fuss about age anyway?

After the table had been cleared, a green baize cloth was laid on it and the board for the game produced. It was a kind of miniature billiards. There was a special 'lady's cue' with a little wooden block on the end. Robert was flattered by having to share the 'gentleman's cue' with Mr Wilkie. The older women played for politeness' sake, with stiff awkward gestures, sitting down between their turns, but Catherine was good at games, and now, darting round the table, her white dress lighting up the sombre room, she played her strokes as skilfully as she could, eager to win even this ridiculous game. It developed into a duel between her and Mr Wilkie, but in the end she won, and went back to the sitting-room in a little glow of triumph.

But in the absence of Mr Wilkie, who was putting away the game, and as the ladies settled down to discuss recipes, boredom struck again. She nudged Robert and whispered:

'Fossils.'

So when Mr Wilkie came back, Robert said politely:

'May we look at the fossils, please?'

Mr Wilkie looked at his wife.

'If you spread a newspaper on the carpet, you may look at them in the dining-room.' She turned to Catherine. 'Mr Wilkie keeps his fossils in the wash-house. But this is a special occasion and I know Robert likes to see them. Your aunts and I will have a nice talk here.'

Mr Wilkie found an old newspaper and while Catherine spread it on the carpet in the dining-room, Robert helped Mr Wilkie carry through the fossils, jumbled up in wooden boxes. Robert began showing off as he lifted them out, for he had, from repeated visits, learned the names.

'Good boy,' said Mr Wilkie. 'I'm glad to see you have remembered things.'

'I'd like you to tell me about the fossils,' said Catherine. 'You would do it much better than Robert.'

So Mr Wilkie brought from the glass-fronted bookcase two volumes full of pictures of fossils and what they had been when alive. He began showing the illustrations to Catherine and identifying the fossils in his box, which were mostly of small fishy creatures. Robert who knew it all already became absorbed in the second volume, largely devoted to satisfyingly monstrous dinosaurs, and stopped listening to Mr Wilkie's gentle voice.

Catherine showed much interest and Tom Wilkie lost his stiffness, talking of belemnites and ammonites. Enthusiasm lit up his face, made him young, and Catherine gave him a smile as he dropped a sea-urchin into her waiting hands. She turned the fossil over with careful fingers, scarcely hearing what he said, thinking it was sad that he should be tied to that starchy creature his wife. How could it have happened? She put down the sea-urchin and interrupted his description of a nautiloid.

'What made you begin collecting fossils?'

Tom Wilkie was silent for a moment.

'I don't really know.'

'You must know. To collect all these ... You must know.'

He groped for words, unused to talk on this level.

'I saw fossils in a museum in London. And then one day I found one in the quarry, and in a field. I bought this book, and discovered there were lots of fossils round here ... '

He glanced at her searching for any sign of derision or contempt. But no, her eyes were serious and attentive. He went on:

'And they're wonderful I think. To have endured so long; ... And then, to think this was once the sea — the water and tides washing over where we are now, and these creatures — that urchin you're holding in your hand being alive in the water ... '

'That's like poetry,' said Catherine.

Tom looked sharply at her. No, she was not mocking him. He remembered from long ago a sneering voice 'Quite the poet aren't we?' and felt again the stab. Into the silence came Robert's voice:

'I wish you could find a bit of a dinosaur, Mr Wilkie. They're more interesting than little fishes.'

Tom smiled, relieved and yet sorry at the interruption. 'I don't think that's likely, Robert. You'll have to go to London to see dinosaurs; in the Natural History Museum.'

Catherine began arranging the fossils in groups on the newspaper.

'They look nice like that, all in order. Couldn't you get a place with shelves where you could lay them out for people to see, not have them all mixed up in a box?'

'Mrs Wilkie doesn't like them in the house. They collect dust. They're lumps of stone you know.'

'They're not,' cried Robert. 'They're special, because they were once alive. Haven't you told Mrs Wilkie?'

He stopped. Mr Wilkie's face was flushing and Robert felt himself grow hot. He had said something wrong. But Catherine saved him.

'The fossils are very interesting and I'd like to find one. Could you show us where to look, Mr Wilkie?'

'If you and Robert like to come out with me tomorrow evening we could look.'

'That would be lovely, wouldn't it Robert? Now we must help Mr Wilkie to put the fossils away.'

She began carefully laying the belemnites in the bottom of a box, covered them with paper and then laid the sea-urchins and so on till all was neatly arranged. Then Mr Wilkie and Robert carried them back to the wash-house. When they came back to the dining-room Catherine had moved into the sunlight shining through the window and her body was a dark shape under her loose white dress. Mr Wilkie stopped so abruptly that Robert bumped into him. Catherine moved into the shade and said:

'I think the others are getting ready to go.'

It was agreed that the following evening Mr Wilkie, Catherine and Robert would meet at the quarry; and there he was waiting for them carrying a geologist's hammer and with a bag over his shoulder. He warned them they must not be too hopeful of finding anything in the chalk-pit, locally known as the quarry, which he had pretty well explored, but the field above had been recently ploughed and there might be something there.

It was a sultry evening of stillness and sunlight. The furrows were dusty and hard to walk on. It was not what Catherine had imagined fossil-hunting would be. She looked at her companions. Robert, head down, now and then stooping to pick up something and then discard it, was clearly absorbed. Mr Wilkie, also walking with head bowed seemed equally absorbed. Catherine began to feel bored and cross.

But Tom Wilkie was totally unaware of his surroundings momentarily even unaware of the girl tramping the furrows so close to him. He was years away, back in that disastrous time in London when Gertrude's sympathy and kindness had been the only good things in life. She had welcomed him back in the evening, drawn him out, listened to his account of the dreary day's doings. She had been like a kind aunt. Then one night she had come to his bed. The next day he found himself engaged to be married. The wedding took place shortly after. He had been trapped, of course. Gertrude was a dutiful wife; kept the house beautifully; 'looked after him'. She hated the farm and all that went with it. They shared no interests. It was life in a well-organised ice-box.

But not until yesterday, and Catherine kneeling by his fossils, Catherine in the sunlight from the window, had he known how bleak, how chill, the ice-box was.

There was a shout from Robert. He had found something — a fossil shell. What was it? Tom identified it as a nautiloid. Now that they had found something, did they want to go on?

Robert did, but Catherine insisted on going back to the quarry. Here it was hot, the level evening sunlight bouncing off the chalk. Sitting on the turf at the top, Robert watched Catherine scrambling about. He thought she was being silly; he knew she was sure-footed as a deer, yet she kept saying she was slipping and asking Mr Wilkie to give her a hand. But she did spy a sea-urchin in the chalk, and with cries that she must get it herself, and balancing on a tangle of fallen turf and brambles she chipped round it. But as she reached up and grasped it, she slipped and would have fallen on her back, if Mr Wilkie had not caught her. He put her down very quickly — he probably thinks she's being silly too, thought Robert — then the two of them joined Robert. Catherine had brought apples, and as they sat and munched them, Robert chattered on about fossils.

'I wish we could find a bit of a dinosaur. Or supposing a fossil came alive. Supping a pterodactyl came flying from the trees — or — or a brontosaurus came barging through the wood — or if even my little shell came alive ... '

'Don't be silly,' said Catherine tartly, clearly not interested in fantasy. But Mr Wilkie in his kind way answered seriously:

'I don't think a fossil would be happy coming back to life. Everything would be completely strange and different and frightening. It would probably just die.'

'I suppose so,' said Robert. 'Anyway, I'm going to look for more shells.'

He jumped up and went back to the ploughed land. Half-way across the field he found another shell and hurried back to the quarry to show his prize. He was ready to shout his triumph as soon as the others came in sight. But the words died in his mouth.

Mr Wilkie had Catherine in his arms and was kissing her — kissing her with short jerky movements of his head — on her lips; her cheeks, her throat — he even buried his face in her hair. And leaning back on her elbows she was accepting it all, though he was almost on top of her. Then as the boy watched in bewildered astonishment, Tom Wilkie suddenly dropped the girl, snatched his bag and hammer and ran along the edge of the field to Steadens.

Robert came slowly down the slope to Catherine and stood staring at her. She was still leaning on her elbows, flushed, biting her lip. She didn't look at him for a moment or two. Then she snapped:

'Why are you looking at me like that?'

'You — Mr Wilkie! He was kissing you.'

'Yes. I made him kiss me.'

'You made him?' His voice rose to a squeak of surprise.

She looked up. To his deeper bewilderment, it seemed as she might be going to cry. Instead she jumped to her feet.

'I made a fossil come alive.'

She almost spat the words at him. And she was away, running down the field towards home.

He caught up with her at the farmyard gate. He was shaking, half-crying, aware that something important had happened not knowing what, her last words to him making her feel implicated.

Catherine caught his arm and squeezed it.

'You must never, ever, tell a living soul what you saw. Swear?'

He was only too ready. 'I swear.'

The post-girl brought the news next morning. There had been an accident. Mr Wilkie had been found with gun-shot wounds beside a stile leading to a spinney where he often went to shoot rabbits. He must have tripped crossing the stile and the gun had gone off. Mr Wilkie was dead.

Catherine and Robert slipped away unheeded from the babble of exclamations and distress down to the river that flowed past the garden. Catherine put her hand into the pocket of her dress and drew out the sea-urchin she had found in the quarry. She flung it into the dark water and it sank into the silt and was lost once more. And in time their guilt sank too, silted over, and became no more than a little nodule of unease and shame.

BETTE LINDSAY HOUSTON

THE FAIRIN

The time has come when I must repossess myself. For the past two weeks — since the day of the funeral — I have belonged to Helen. Tying off and sealing up her life, I have abdicated the rule of my own affairs: resigned the separate authority I held to so stubbornly during all the years of our friendship.

Helen had neither brother nor sister, and she named me in her will as sole executor. So I did what had to be done: packed up her clothes and passed on the parcels to the charity shop to which we had both given an afternoon a week; the mountain of manuscripts, I took apart, sorted and collated; finally, and with averted mind, I abandoned to black plastic sacks, the unusable leavings of her fifty years.

Through it all I have been haunted by my own guilt, my treachery.

Which is ridiculous. Guilt does not come into the situation. I have betrayed no one.

Except yourself. The soft voice. The unrelenting tone. I close my mind to this echo, this ghost.

I have great need to separate myself from the past. But my imagination, operating like a faulty magic lantern, continues to throw a random selection of images onto the screen behind my eyes.

Especially and repeatedly, there is a picture that draws me back fifteen years, to the house at Mearnock, the place where my marriage had its limited existence. I see myself standing in the garden there on a still, silent morning of fuzzy grey light . . .

It was December. There were no flowers left, and the last of the leaves had been burned. But my conscientious little winter-flowering cherry tree was cupolaed in frail pale blossom. I was standing looking at this fragile flourish when Helen came in by the back gate.

'The flat next door to ours is for sale,' she said. 'Are you interested?'

I stretched out my hand and stroked the tree's shiny trunk. There were no gardens down in Gracie Street where Helen and her husband lived. No trees, even.

'Oh yes,' I said. 'I am interested.'

I had to be. My divorce had gone through, and Gerry, married to his new love, had put our house up for sale. And my allotted income would provide but sparingly for me and my boys, my ten-year-old twins. I should have to change my style of living; I should have to find a way of earning money.

'We'd better ring up right now,' Helen said. 'Act — that is the way to get yourself fit to tackle the future.'

And, once we were settled in Gracie Street, Helen risked a further piece of advice.

'Have you thought of taking up writing again, Irene? Strongly therapeutic, you know. You could clear Gerry from your system once and for all if you wrote out the whole story, from beginning to end.'

The idea appealed, and soon I was snatching every possible minute to bury myself in a task which must have answered an existential need, so completely did it hold my mind in thrall.

Helen was delighted and approving — until I gave her the first part of my manuscript to read. Then her eyes took on a watchful, disappointed expression. She said nothing; but the nothing was eloquent.

She had reckoned without the uncertainties of my nature. Her talent was austere and true. Mine — for what it was worth — was wayward. Once my imagination had woven its own thread through the Gerry story, a fairy tale was created. A sophisticated fairy tale: a saleable, wish-fulfilling romance.

It was my good fortune that when I had completed the novel to my own satisfaction, I posted it to Martin and Leigh. John Martin saw something he liked in that first story, and, because he realized I could be drilled into achieving a steady output, he sat down with me, and showed me how to re-shape the book to make it a commercial proposition. So I acquired a career which enabled me to put jam on our bread, and cream on our cakes, without having to absent myself from home; my boys had it both ways: no latch key, no deprivation.

For Helen, writing was a vocation. After the publication of that first novel, she detached herself from my stories.

But, strangely, she allowed me to be involved in hers. She trusted my judgment she said; always gave me her first draft to read.

'Spot the errors,' she would say.

This was a daunting demand. To my eyes and mind, her style was flawless — balanced and sensuous, with every word in the right place; every shade of meaning clear and exact.

But the important quality in her stories — their dominant virtue — was a reality-rooted integrity which offered the thrill of recognition to the reader of similar experience, and gave true understanding to the others.

The only kind of criticism I made concerned the rare hiatus.

'*Why* did Jennifer loathe her brother?' I would say. 'This character's phobia about the police, how did it arise?' I would ask. That sort of thing.

She would listen, not speaking, her eyes full of thought. And when she showed me the final version, I would find that phrases had been omitted, or new passages inserted. Then I would glow with secret satisfaction. To be even the slightest influence on Helen Broderick — surely that was to merit a footnote in the history of literature.

Nevertheless, I stuck stubbornly to my own way with my own work, romanticizing for all I was worth, and pandering to my readers' need to escape reality. My close involvement with Helen's work, however, did have its effect on me. As the years passed, the texture of my novels deepened, and the quality of my prose improved. But I saw myself always as a craftswoman: whereas Helen was the complete artist.

And with the undeliberate ruthlessness of the dedicated creator, Helen put her art first — gave it prime claim on her time and energy. Tom Broderick saw no fault in this. Twenty years older than his wife, he was inordinately proud of Helen, and showed no discontent with her sketchy house-keeping and plain-to-a-fault cookery.

Easy-going and optimistic — always ready to break out in a smile — Tom Broderick came to represent strength and dependability to us three. And there was never any doubt that the proximity of my boys filled a gap in his life. To Alan and Jamie, he became a beloved companion: he taught them to swim, showed them how to box, and carried them off to carefully selected football matches.

At first, I worried because, as children will, they tended to take his interest in them for granted — made, it seemed to me, outrageous demands on his good nature.

But my misgivings left me on the Saturday set aside for

the building of the bogie.

Helen and I stood laughing on the landing, as the man and the two boys footed it cautiously down to the backyard, their arms clutching planks and tools, their pockets bulging with bags of nails.

As we turned to our separate doorways, Helen said to me, 'I owe you a debt of gratitude. It is because of your two that I have none of the guilt that burdens a childless wife: especially one with a husband who was meant to be a father.'

We had ten of those happy, sharing years. Then Tom died: dropped dead at Helen's feet one summer afternoon.

Only two years after that, the boys graduated, and now Alan is civil-engineering in Canada, and Jamie, a geologist, is with an oil company in Australia.

And Helen is dead. I am alone.

Alone, but alive. And it is with the business of living that I must concern myself.

Today, I have an appointment with John Martin. I sit down at the dressing-table and regard myself: see a haggard face. My eyes seem to have shrunk back in their sockets; my cheeks are drawn; my lips as pale as though I had been drinking neat vinegar.

I assemble my pots and tubes, my brushes and puffs. With the deftness of the well-practised, I apply my salves and powders. When I have finished, my face has a bland bloom, and green shadow has given an illusion of lambency to my eyes.

When I am completely ready, I study my reflection in the full-length looking-glass. I am well enough pleased to give myself a nod. I'll 'do'. I shall hold my own. Even in The Bodega.

Every year, John Martin has a long holiday in Strathglass and, on his way back south, he stops off in Glasgow. And gives me lunch. In The Bodega.

But I needn't be smart-alecky about John Martin. He is no figure of fun in my life.

I take out my diary to note, in my usual meticulous fashion, the various errands I shall do while I am in town. There is the funeral bill to pay. I write 'Undertaker' above John's name. Then I make a shopping list. I write carefully, fitting the letters neatly between the faint blue lines.

(Suddenly, I have a vision of Helen standing with a page of notes in each hand, contrasting my precise italic script with her own open black lettering; she laughs — a short, dry

laugh that I have learned to recognise as a symptom of irritation. I suppose I often plucked at her nerves, with my fussi-
ness over clothes, and my housewifely preoccupations. 'I
wish you would attend to your talent, woman!' she would
cry.)

Time to go. My front door bangs behind me, and I stare
at the nameplate on the door at the other side of the landing.
'H. Broderick'.

'Are you the Helen Broderick who wrote *A Letter from
his Wife*?' Those were the first words I ever spoke to her.
Twenty-one years ago. At some literary party to which I had
been invited on the strength of three published short stories.

'You have said exactly the right thing!' She had a soft,
philosophizing voice, and her smile was self-mocking.

She was not well known. Her stories were not of the best-
selling kind. But discriminating readers and literary folk
thought well of her, and her short stories and poems appeared
in good anthologies. This pleased her. Popularity was unim-
portant. As was money. The appurtenances of contemporary
living hardly existed for Helen. Her attention was fixed on
her muse.

I was unutterably proud to have her for my friend.

A couple of years ago, she had a third novel published,
and it won an award. This piece of recognition seemed to un-
clot her genius. Short stories and poems poured from her in a
cataract of creativity. And she started on the research for a
new novel, with a sweet, tranquil assurance.

It was on the way back from the official presentation of
the award, when we were both in a state of high euphoria,
that she told me about the lump.

'A nuisance,' she called it.

I could not believe that I was understanding her properly.
The thing had been on her breast for months. I stood over
her while she rang her doctor, and went with her to see him
on the day after.

He was an old friend, and sheer shock forced from him an
expression of his outrage that a 'woman of your intelligence'
had not come to him long before.

'I was hoping it might go away,' she said, apologetically.
'I have been so busy. I did not want my attention to be di-
verted.'

The flippancy was mocked by the terror in her eyes.

But as we turned away from the doctor's door, 'That's

the first time he has called me *intelligent*,' she said drily.

   . . . I have been standing staring at that name-plate for
several minutes. Ridiculous. Briskly, I walk down the first
flight of stairs. Then I pause again, to look out through the
stairhead window; the prospect is of backyards and bin-
shelters. In my mind, for the first time for years, I see the
cherry tree in the garden at Mearnock: and I know that without my sons, without Helen, I do not wish to go on living in
this place.

   Now there surfaces in my consciousness, the telephone
conversation I had with John Martin on the day before Helen
went into hospital for the last time. He had rung up about
the manuscript I had posted to him a week or two earlier.
This was the novel I had written during the months when we
believed that the disease was conquered: an insulated, fecund
period, during which Helen took time off from pondering the
new novel, and produced three short stories of uncanny brilli-
ance.

   But by the time John called me, all that was over, and
there was no space in my mind for his words. Now, however,
I recall something about possible American publication. My
thoughts tremble, and I run down the remaining steps to the
street.

   The undertaker's office is all light wood and chintzy curtains. Incongruous, but well-intentioned.

   The man who took compassionate charge at Helen's
funeral comes in while I am writing the cheque, and recog-
nizes me.

   'Feeling better?'

   I shrug.

   He puts a hand lightly on my shoulders.

   'I must say that I admired the way you stuck to your
principles.'

   'What do you mean?'

   'Having no minister, and no hymns.'

   Ah! But I had wished for both, to come between me and
the fearsome reality of the coffin. It was Helen's principles
that had been honoured.

   'The organist and I were glad of the change,' he goes on;
chattily. 'Your friend's was the sixth funeral we had had that
day, and after five doses of "By Cool Siloam", and "Crim-
ond", your Bach and Dvorak were like a tonic.'

A giggle bursts from me. Helen would have put this man into a story.

'Ach, but I like you Glasgow folk,' he says. 'I'm from Dundee, but the twenty years I have spent as an undertaker in Glasgow have been the best years of my life.'

'It's great to be happy in your work,' I say. *I* say? Those are Helen's words, spoken in her dry, impassive tone. It is as though she nudged me.

If I do not take a grip of myself, I shall develop into a thorough-going neurotic.

Helen is dead.

Outside on the pavement, I look at my watch, take my mind back to John Martin.

He is waiting for me. I feel a rush of affection. He must be nearly sixty now, but his backbone is still strictly perpendicular, and the extra flesh brought by the years, is distributed evenly over his broad frame. He knows what I like, and my drink stands ready on the bar.

As I raise myself onto a stool, I get the feeling that I am at the end of a long spell of hard labour; or that I am convalescing after an illness. John has always had — and used — the power to put heart in me.

Over lunch, he chats about the weather up north, and describes every fish he claims to have caught — or nearly caught. He tells a good story about his ghillie. He always has a good story about his ghillie.

At the coffee stage, the climate changes. Now, we are on the breezy uplands of business talk. John's eyes quiz me over the rim of his brandy glass.

'How would you like to be a wealthy woman?'

'Very much. That is why I do the pools.'

'Never mind the quips. If you will put in some extra work — hard work — on this book, we can make it into something big. I am practically certain I can sell it to America. In which case we shall give it a big hype; aim for the top of the best-sellers list.'

I listen. I glow, and float.

'But everything,' John says severely, 'depends on America. And to make it more attractive over there, I want you to weave in some episodes set in the States.'

I burst out laughing. Then pull myself together very smartly. This is my cherry tree we are talking about.

'Of course. Whatever you say, John.'

The novel is the story of a Glasgow family, covering the

years from 1913 to 1927. I found the background, and the germ of the plot, when I was helping Helen with the research for the book she did not live to write.

'Which part of America?' I say.

John has thought about this. 'Pittsburgh.'

We get down to details: decide which member of the family should emigrate, and where the extra chapters can best be inserted. John and I have worked together for so many years, that we are able to communicate in a kind of verbal shorthand.

'This could be the first of a trilogy,' John says eventually.

I see what he means, and am elated beyond anything I have felt since the twins graduated.

He goes off to collect his luggage, and I tackle my shopping. Camembert, I buy, and lapsang souchong; fresh salmon; asparagus and strawberries; and two dozen yellow roses. Then I hail a taxi. To Hell with poverty. I am a potential best-seller.

At six o'clock, a dealer is coming to Helen's flat to value her furniture. I make a pot of tea; carry the smoky liquid to my desk.

I take out a new exercise book, and lift my silver, narrow-nibbed pen, my instrument of creation.

The work goes well. I am confident, and, therefore, competent. By half-past-five, I have planned the new chapters, and made notes of changes to be made in the manuscript as it stands.

I go into the hall, and lift the loop of chain which shackles Helen's keys to mine. But at the open door, I shiver, and turn back, to take from the hall chest, the crimson stole she gave to me a dozen Christmases ago.

Her flat has lost its body scent. It has the neutral stony smell of a dwelling deserted. In the living-room, I kneel before the gas fire and throw the switch. There is a burp, then heat, and a glow which changes the walls from white to pale rose.

I sit in my usual chair, facing the one that was hers. I wrap the stole tightly around me, gripping myself, feeling my ribs under my fingertips. This is a keening posture, but I am not here to cry. I have never wept for Helen. When we were fighting the cancer, there was no energy to spare — all was needed to sustain the edifice of optimism: and I have found no well of tears in the arid blankness of defeat.

The last time Helen and I faced each other here was six

weeks ago: the middle of July; Glasgow Fair Monday; and
the eve of the day when she was to go back into hospital for
the new treatment — the treatment that so nearly succeeded.

She was up, and dressed, that night. In navy slacks and a
tunic the colour of bluebells, she was putting on a brave show
for her visitors. (We had the idea that if you make people
think optimistically about you, beneficial vibrations result.)

Paul and Mary Connor were old, fondly regarded friends.
Thoughtful and perceptive, they did not wait long. As they
took their leave, Helen's lips slipped into a half-smile.

'Pray for me,' said Helen the agnostic to her Catholic
friends.

When I came back, after seeing them to the door, Helen
said. 'It was good of them to come.' Then, apologetically,
she added, 'But it is so restful when it is just you.'

We sat gazing at each other.

'Do I sense happy thoughts, Irene?'

I managed a smile.

'I am sitting here gloating over you, and thanking my
lucky star that I said the right thing that first evening!'

'Golden moment!' she said. 'You made my fantasizing
come to pass.' She leaned back in her chair; amusement
curled her lips and put brightness in her eyes: ' "Are you the
Helen Broderick who wrote . . . " *The* Helen Broderick!'

'Pretty good', I said, 'considering that it was by the
merest fluke that I had read your novel!'

We laughed together. And, astonishingly, the laughter
exalted us: for one illuminated moment, we understood all
experience — and were able to accept it. Briefly, sharply, we
shared — worldlessly but manifestly — an illusion of all-
knowingness.

A few peaceful seconds passed, then Helen spoke.

'I have something on my mind . . . ' Her voice wobbled;
faded.

'What?'

'Oh, nothing new.' Her look was at once appealing — and
stern.

'Look, now that you have no one dependent on you,
wouldn't you find it in your heart to make the material sacri-
fice? Earn less. Give yourself up to real writing?'

'You know I'd do anything for you, Helen: anything
within the bounds of possibility. But I am not capable of
your kind of writing. For a start, I hate and fear austerity.
And my talent is a weak and feeble thing compared to yours.'

'You have never put it to the test.'

'Helen — dear. I want to please you. But there must be no lies between us.'

'It's just that you have done so much for me. It would have been lovely if you'd have let me show you a better way. Give you a kind of fairin.'

I laughed — seized on the word as a means of escape.

' "Fairin" is right,' I said. 'You were the one who pointed out to me that it would take the Scots tongue to invent a word which can mean either a gift or a highly salutary punishment.

> "Ah, Tam! ah Tam! thou'll get thy fairin!
> In hell they'll roast thee like a herrin!"

Fairin indeed!'

Helen laughed with me, then leaned over and touched the back of my hand.

'Nevertheless,' she said, 'the subject is not closed!'

'Now, how about a cup of tea, Helen? Or would you like coffee?'

'Let's have whisky,' she said. 'Just for devilment.'

The liquid gleamed like a topaz as I raised my glass.

'Here's to THE GREAT GLASGOW NOVEL!'

This was our jokey name for her new book. Half-in-fun, wholly-in-earnest as far as I was concerned. And a little bit with her, too, maybe.

'Here's to you,' she said. 'A big thanks for everything. Especially that help with the research. I could never have managed without you.'

'All grist to the mill,' I said.

The engrossed tranquillity of those page-turning library mornings had belonged to another world. Fragile, musty newsprint had made a present of the past to me, as, with a delightful sense of discovery, I fingered leaves printed before I was born.

'I do hope I live to write it, Irene. All I have ever wanted is a short row of published work. To show that I have been here. It is the knowledge of the books I could still write that makes the threat of death so unbearable.'

'You'll write your books, my dear,' I said. I spoke with hope, not hypocrisy. The specialist had been encouraging about the new drug.

'I choose to believe you,' she said. 'I choose to believe you.'

The doorbell rings; a summons to the present.

This is the dealer. He is a dour man with a sullen flat face. And he has but one line. He utters it in every room. 'No market for stuff like this.' He would say the same in face of an array of Chippendale.

At the end of his tour of inspection, we stand by the piano. On top of it, there lie, a blue folder, some notebooks, and a bundle of fibre-tipped pens — things I had brought back from the hospital. I had forgotten they were here.

When Helen was worried or depressed — or when the right words would not come — she used to play herself out of the doldrums. She was a better-than-fair pianist, and Bach was the well from which she drew refreshment for her daemon. Then, when her mind became repopulated with images, her lips would lift in a smile, and she would strike up her own saucy version of *Highland Laddie*. After that, she would go back to her desk.

'As for this,' the dealer slaps the lid, 'you'll have to pay me to take it away.'

I glare at him.

Oh, go to Hell!

'I wish to keep the piano,' I say, wondering where I shall find a place for it.

'Up to you. As for the rest . . . ' He mentions a figure which, I realize, is ridiculously low. I should do battle — for the sake of the beneficiary, old Mrs Broderick, Tom's mother; and to demonstrate to this man that I am not a fool.

But, conquered by the bitter sadness of the situation, I shrug. 'All right,' I say, and arrange a day and hour with him.

He has gone. I lift the blue folder, open it. It contains the notes we made on those cocooned library mornings: her bold black lettering interleaved with my careful script. I riffle through the pages, and come to a sheaf of leaves clipped together under a covering sheet which has CHAPTER ONE scrawled flourishingly across it.

This must have been written in hospital. I lean my elbows on the piano top, and read.

At the end, I drop my head till my brow touches the grave-cold paper.

Helen's prose had always been dynamic, and her images evocative; but with death at her shoulder, she had found an extra dimension, opened up her talent to its spell-binding uttermost.

This chapter — this beginning — is lit with fires of urgency and passion. It bears the thumb print of an artist who has reached maturity.

I press the folder to my breasts, and turn away from Helen's home.

My own work awaits me. I sit down at my desk, read what I wrote an hour ago, and lift my pen.

But my mind does not vibrate; my fingers are rigid, and the pen is immobile. I let it drop, and take one from Helen's bundle.

Immediately, virtue returns to me.

Damn it. Damn. Damn. Damn.

I know what my unconscious is up to — making me head up a clean sheet with these two words. I know what has happened. Oh yes. I have got my fairin, that's what.

A cascade of tears spills from my eyes. No cherry tree for me, now. Or ever. God help me — God help me a lot — sniffing and sobbing and cursing, I am engaged in writing, in bold open black lettering, THE GREAT GLASGOW NOVEL.

STANLEY ROGER GREEN

SKATING ON DUNSAPIE

Dunsapie Loch, said to be bottomless,
Is where I describe circles
Each ice-bound winter
Over a hole that plunges down
To Earth's turbulent centre,
If what they say is true.

Or even further, by a stretch
Of the mind's telescoping eye,
To a billabong in Australia —
No less than the distance between
One and another, or you and I —
And there a girl may be swimming

Under my feet, and eucalyptus trees,
Her limbs clenching, unfolding
Around a flexing solar plexus,
Her navel linked to my tunnel vision
Forming a personal singular axis,
A polarity of heat and ice.

By this we are bound, and bound
To be vulnerable in a turbulent world
Looking vainly for its calm centre;
She breast-stroking between water-lilies
And banks of golden wattle
With never a thought for winter,

Myself circling, looking for an opening,
Afraid of what I may not find.
If what they say is true,
Bottomless too is the outstretched mind;
But we only strive to reach the other side
And hope the thin ice will not break.

NORMAN KREITMAN

DESIGNING A JAPANESE GARDEN

First you must ask disturbing questions;
do you, for example, insist on walking about
    or have you acquired
enough understanding to stay in one place?

Then consider purpose. Presumably the garden
will chiefly be used for poetry competitions,
    or will you drink tea,
or instead, think of the verities of the Masters?

Decide next on what is within, what is out,
how light shall enter the eye of the house
    when shadows lean outwards,
where the floor will end and the world begin.

And clarify your thoughts concerning the open air;
need you borrow space from the hazy mountains
    or is the nearer sky enough?
Would a wall help to block and organise your seeing?

Then you may set your garden, but choose to show
chiefly those truths which are assymetrical;
    pain need not appear
but have water for balm, rushes for consolation.

    Finally, place the massive stone,
    and let that be your gravity.

TRIAL OF THE ELDERS

The clever judge had twitched away the thin deceit
　　revealing their needs
as if the hangdog pair had publicly confessed.
　　Then the abuse began,
grew in the crowd's throat to a chant of revenge.

But though they flinched for cover yet in the skull
　　two visions still embraced.
One was of sunlight fingering the ripples of the pool
　　with the underside of rushes
repeating the scintillation, and then green echoes

filtering up through the willows, a trellis made
　　of leaves against the sky.
This was the place, a setting like a jewelled frame.

But the second vision was sight's centre, the image
　　of how a woman might stand
as if up to her knees in water, with limbs draped
　　in the line of her tresses
and the planes of skin light against her own shadow.

Such harmony had waited lurking within their eyes
　　since long before the day
Susanna stepped into her picture. And as they aged
　　the vision gleamed more brightly
to haunt their skinny limbs like the distant fact of youth,
leading them now to death, carried like breath to the end.

EWAN R. McVICAR

HOUSE PARTY COUNTRY

A reel of pornographs
Chased by Brian Rix's trousers
Dashed down the driveway.

Lady Caroline
Spent her afternoons in the morning room
And her evenings in the way of the family.

A visiting diplomat from High Dudgeon
Sulked in the scullery
Skulked in the shrubbery
Shrugged off encouragement
And entered a nunnery.
Which engendered a sex-role incident.

The battling butler and the chamfered
chambermaid serenaded the crusty cook
with 'Pail Hands I loved,'
and such music-hall delights as
Qu. How do you approach a
cockroach?
An. With caution.
  And a meat mallet.

The mellow gardener
Gave the lady of the house
A huge cucumber,
Seedless.

Unnoticed,
The house itself, seeking support,
Took honest employment
As part of the National Truss.

THINGS I WISH I STILL HAD

The snap-on sunglasses that catapulted out of
the car window somewhere upcountry from Mombasa.

Dark hair.

The umbrella I bought in a Left Luggage sale, and
left in a London folk club the same night.

The work address of Alison, the only hairdresser
I ever trusted.

Belief that democracy can work.

The Moroccan iron scorpion I used to place on
my bed-side table.

Belief that communism can work.

The soft cover for my camera.

The partners to all those odd socks.

The East African pop records I left in a
trunk stored in the vaults of the National and
Grindlay's Bank Ltd, Aden, shortly before the
Arabs occupied Crater, and about which the
Bank never answered my letters.

Everything else that was in that trunk.

Trust in other drivers.

The lens cover for my camera.

The review in *Record Mirror* of the first
song I wrote.

Non-nicotine-stained fingers.

The books I've lent.

The records I've lent.

Belief that there is a God.

The crystal-clear understanding of the world
and all its doings that came to me one drunk
night in 1982.

A more selective memory.

NOTES ON CONTRIBUTORS

JANET CAIRD was born in Nyasaland where her father was an educational missionary. She was educated at Dollar Academy, the Universities of Edinburgh and Grenoble, and the Sorbonne. She trained as a teacher and in 1938 married James B. Caird, HMIS. She lives in Inverness. She has published six novels, one children's book and two collections of poetry.

ROBERT CRAWFORD was born in 1959 in Glasgow. A graduate of Glasgow and Oxford, he is now a Junior Research Fellow at St Hugh's College, Oxford. Recent poems in Scots and English have appeared in *Cencrastus, Lines Review, London Magazine, NWS, Sterts and Stobies* and *Verse*. There have been articles in various learned journals and a study of T.S. Eliot is forthcoming from OUP.

MAUD DEVINE was born in 1948 in Glasgow, and belongs to it. She was educated at Glasgow University and is now a mobile librarian, hoping for a re-schedule to the seaside. She started writing three years ago, but the one poem hitherto accepted for publication has since gone missing.

THOMAS F. DOCHERTY was born in Glasgow in 1938 and went to school and university there. He teaches English in a large comprehensive school in the city.

PAT GERBER, itinerant Glaswegian since 1934, survived school, married, mothered and matured. Langside College gave her Highers. After struggling through an Honours M.A., the fifth baby and divorce she worked in Further Education. Then Cyril Gerber kindly marrried her and encouraged her to 'work' less and write more. Her first published stories were in *NWS* 3.

ENID GAULDIE has been a full-time writer since 1969 and has published *Cruel Habitations* (1974), *The Scottish Country Miller* (1981), and has had stories in Collins' *Scottish Short Stories 1984* and *1985*. A novel is forthcoming. She lives in Invergowrie, near Dundee.

MARY GLADSTONE was born in England of Scottish parents and has lived almost all of her life in Scotland except for being schooled in Bristol. She studied drama at the Royal Scottish Academy of Music and Drama and now teaches part-time for the Extra-mural Department of Edinburgh University. She reviews books and occasionally theatre for *The Scotsman*. She has published and broadcast a number of short stories and had her first play performed at the Traverse in March 1985.

ELIZABETH GOWANS was born in Edinburgh in 1936 to a shepherding family from the Pentlands. She was educated in Greenock and at Glasgow University in languages and is an ex-teacher and pre-school adviser. Other publications: *The Stravaigers* (Hamish Hamilton 1984, to appear soon as *Shepherd's Flock* from Magnet), *Shepherd's Warning* (HH 1985), *Sleeping Warrior* (HH October 1986), and stories in Collins' *Scottish Short Stories 1981, 1982* and *1984*.

STANLEY ROGER GREEN was born in Edinburgh not too recently. Schooled variously in Edinburgh and Clackmannanshire, he was sidetracked into Leith Nautical College before completing formal education at Edinburgh College of Art as an architect. He has travelled widely as cadet seaman, soldier, student and architect. Author of about 100 poems, some of which have appeared in *NWS* 2 and 3, and the collection *A Suburb of Belsen* (Paul Harris, 1977), only a dozen of his stories have yet been published: but one was recently broadcast in China. Four plays have been performed.

DOROTHY K. HAYNES was born in Lanark in 1918, and educated there and in Aberlour. She is married with two sons and three grandchildren. She has contributed over many years to many leading publications, short story anthologies, the BBC and *The Scots Magazine*. She has published two novels, an autobiography, and two books of short stories, and has completed a novel about New Lanark.

BETTE LINDSAY HOUSTON was born in Glasgow and educated at Strathbungo School and at commercial college. While working as a secretary, she continued to chase after learning in extra-mural classes. She lived for several years in Dublin, where she discovered how to write, and has now published many short stories and articles, and has broadcast.

Married, with a daughter, she now lives happily in Glasgow, and is engaged on a novel.

NORMAN KREITMAN is a doctor who has a research post in Edinburgh where he has lived for many years. His work has appeared in various magazines and anthologies. The publication of his first book *Touching Rock* is currently being negotiated, and a second collection is approaching completion.

MAURICE LINDSAY was born in Glasgow in 1918. Seven years in the army, he has been music critic of *The Bulletin*, radio and television broadcaster, Programme Controller of Border Television and Director of the Scottish Civic Trust. He is now honorary Secretary General of Europa Nostra. He has written or edited over fifty books, including *The Burns Encyclopaedia, History of Scottish Literature, Collected Poems* and his autobiography *Thank You for Having Me*.

IAN McFADYEN was born in Edinburgh in 1950, raised in West Lothian, and educated there, in Peebles and at Edinburgh University. He now lives in Peebles, with wife and daughter, and teaches English in Penicuik. He has published occasional poems in Scottish periodicals and has written, among others, love poems, green poems, and historical poems, some of them in Scots.

IONA McGREGOR was born in 1929 in Aldershot, and spent her childhood defending various parts of the British Empire. She was educated in India, Scotland, England, Wales, and spent most of her working life as a teacher of Classics, (with five years on *D.O.S.T.*). She has published several juvenile historical novels (Scottish backgrounds) for Faber; her latest work is *Wallace and Bruce* (text-book, Oliver and Boyd, 1986). She is now a full-time writer, based in Edinburgh since 1969.

ROSA MACPHERSON was born in Alloa in 1956. She is a trained teacher. In 1985 she won the Radio Scotland Short Story Competition; in the same year she was published in *Edinburgh Review* 7. She is tutor for the Alloa Writing Group.

EWAN R. McVICAR was born in Inverness in 1941. He has been banker in Africa, guitar teacher in USA, social worker in Scotland. He had a song in the Top Twenty in 1959. Songs, poetry, prose — on radio, TV, disc, peace demos — and in *The Scotsman, Edinburgh Review, Orbis, Literarisches Arbeitsjournal* etc. He says: 'I write songs for other people and poetry for myself.'

PAT MOSEL, a Scottish Borderer (born in 1951 in Bulawayo, Zimbabwe) has Journalism and B.A. Hons (English) degrees. She has had newspaper and magazine articles published internationally, has edited specialist supplements and contributed to the Roxburghshire section of the *Third Statistical Account of Scotland*, which is still to be published. She is married, with two children. 'Seasons' was written in East Africa.

PETER WOOD MOWAT was born in Portknockie in 1951. He left in 1969 'to mis-spend' his youth in Aberdeen. He is married with two children, works in engineering administration, and lives in Inverbervie. He has had a long apprenticeship in writing but only in the past year has he published outwith Aberdeen, with poems in *Lines Review*, and a short story and poems in *Chapman*.

ANNE ROSS MUIR was born in Aberdeen. After graduating with an M.A. in English Literature from Aberdeen University, she went to the U.S. where she completed an M.Sc. in television and film production. After ten years in the States, she returned to Scotland where she now works as a free-lance writer/producer/director.

MICHAEL MUNRO was born in Glasgow (where he still lives) in 1954. He was educated at Allan Glen's and at Glasgow University. He is an editor with Collins, and is married, with one daughter. He is the author of *The Patter*, a best-selling dictionary of Glasgow dialect.

WILMA MURRAY was born in 1939 near Inverurie. She was educated at Inverurie Academy and Aberdeen University. She taught in schools for several years before joining Aberdeen College of Education as a lecturer in Geography. Her stories have been published in *The Scottish Review, Chapman, Cencrastus, The Scotsman* and *NWS* among others, and broadcast by Radio Okney and Radio Forth.

ROLAND PORTCHMOUTH was born in London in 1923. He served in the Royal Navy 1942-6 and was an art teacher and lecturer in teacher training colleges 1951-68. He is the author of art books and of a children's novel. Religious paintings by him are permanently mounted in Peebles Old Parish Church and poems are regularly published in *Life and Work*. He is a Church of Scotland minister in Perthshire.

IAN RANKIN was born in Cardenden, Fife in 1960. He is a prize-winning short-story writer, and his work has appeared in *NWS* 2 and 3, Collins' *Scottish Short Stories 1986*, *The Scotsman*, *Scottish Review* and elsewhere, and stories have been broadcast on BBC Radio 4 and Radio Forth. His first novel, *The Flood*, appeared in 1986, and his second novel, *Knots and Crosses* will be published by Bodley Head in 1987.

LAURNA ROBERTSON was born in Shetland, and educated at Aberdeen University. She now lives in Edinburgh and works as a teacher.

DILYS ROSE was born in Glasgow in 1954 and now lives in Edinburgh. Poems, stories and reviews have been published in various magazines and anthologies, and stories have been broadcast on Radio 3 and 4. She was awarded a writer's bursary by the Scottish Arts Council in 1985.

IAIN CRICHTON SMITH was born in Lewis in January 1928. He was educated in the Nicolson Institute, Stornoway, and Aberdeen University. He taught English in secondary school till 1977, when he took up full-time writing. He has written poems, novels, short stories and plays in both Gaelic and English.

HARRIET SMYTH was born in Kirkcaldy in 1942, educated at Kirkcaldy High School then trained as a teacher at Moray House. She presently teaches adults with a mental handicap. She spent her early married years in Glasgow, and now lives in Linlithgow with her husband and three children. She was runner-up in the 1984 Radio Forth Short Story Competition.

GAVIN SPROTT was born in Dundee in 1943. His father was an Episcopalian clergyman and his mother an artist. He was at school in Dundee and a boarding school in England which he disliked and contrived to leave at 15. He took a variety of jobs until he entered further education and read Scottish history at Edinburgh. He has since worked in the Country Life Section of the National Museum in Edinburgh.

DERICK THOMSON was born in Stornoway in 1921. Educated at the Nicolson Institute, Aberdeen University, Cambridge University and University College, Bangor, he has lectured at Edinburgh, Aberdeen and Glasgow. Professor of Celtic at Glasgow since 1963, he is author of many books in Gaelic and English, including *Creachadh Na Clarsaich (Collected Poems)*, 1982, and *An Introduction to Gaelic Poetry*, 1974. He has edited *Gairm* since 1952.

RAYMOND VETTESE was born in Arbroath in 1950. He was educated at Montrose Academy and lives in the town. He writes mainly in Scots, and has been published in *Akros, Chapman, Lallans, Radical Scotland, Orbis, Scottish Review* and *Lines*; he appears in the anthology *Four Scottish Poets*. He has made several BBC broadcasts. A collection is scheduled for next year and a cassette under the Scotsoun label is due soon.

JANE WEBSTER was born in Edinburgh in 1956. She studied English at the University of Stirling. 'The Unicorn Dance' is her first published story.

THE ASSOCIATION FOR SCOTTISH LITERARY STUDIES

The Association for Scottish Literary Studies exists to promote the study, teaching and writing of Scottish literature, and to further the study of the languages of Scotland. It was founded in 1970 by members of the Scottish Universities, and is now an international organisation, with members in 22 countries.

The ASLS fulfils its aims of promoting the study, teaching and writing of Scottish literature and of furthering the study and the use of the languages of Scotland, by publishing annually an edited text of Scottish literature, scholarly journals, and *New Writing Scotland*. It also produces materials for use in schools, texts for students and other publications.

Membership of the ASLS is open to all who support the aims of the Association and who pay an annual subscription. Please address enquiries to:

Association for Scottish Literary Studies
c/o Department of English
University of Aberdeen
Aberdeen AB9 2UB

Honorary Members

Norman MacCaig, Sorley MacLean, Naomi Mitchinson
Edwin Morgan, David Murison, Iain Crichton Smith

Officers
President: Thomas Crawford, University of Aberdeen
Past President: Professor David Daiches, University of Edinburgh
Secretary: Dr David Robb, University of Dundee
Treasurer: Dr David Hewitt, University of Aberdeen
General Editor: Dr Douglas Mack, University of Stirling
Language Committee Convener: Derrick McClure, University of Aberdeen

The ASLS is in receipt of subsidy from the Scottish Arts Council